HOW TO LIVE BY THE QUR'AN

Discover the Power of the Quran: A Guide to Living a Fulfilling Life

Akhlaque Ahmed

Akhlaque Ahmed

HOW TO LIVE BY THE QUR'AN

Discover the Power of the Quran: A Guide to Living a Fulfilling Life

Akhlaque Ahmed

Akhlaque Ahmed

How to Live by The Qur'an

Copyright © by S Akhlaque Ahmed

Published in the Great Britain in 2022 by S Akhlaque Ahmed
at Faithbook London

All rights reserved. No parts of this publication may be reproduced, stored in a retrieval system, or transmitted, in any form or by any means or be used in any manner whatsoever without the prior permission in writing of the publisher, nor by otherwise circulated in any form of binding or cover other than that in which it is published and without a similar condition including this condition being imposed on the subsequent purchaser except for the use of brief quotations in a book review or scholarly journal.

First Printing: December 2022
Printed and bound in Great Britain
Price: Paperback GBP £7.99
Hardcover GBP £11.99

Faithbook London
Smart Print
30 - 32 Watney Market, London E1 2PR

www.faithbooklondon.com

Dedication

To My Mother
Who first introduced me to the Majestic Qur'an

A man came to the Prophet and said, 'O Messenger of Allah! Who among the people is the most worthy of my good companionship?' The Prophet (PBUH) said: Your mother. The man said, 'Then who?' The Prophet said: Then your mother. The man further asked, 'Then who?' The Prophet said: Then your mother. The man asked again, 'Then who?' The Prophet said: Then your father. (Bukhari, Muslim)

Akhlaque Ahmed

How to Live by The Qur'an

Contents

A Note from The Author..x

Acknowledgement...xi

Preface..xii

Introduction..14

1. Introduction to the Quran, Its Core Principles, and Values..18

2. Understanding the Qur'an in a Contemporary Context 22

3. Connecting to the Qur'an and using it as a Source of Guidance..25

4. Living by the Qur'an: A Revelation of Mercy and Compassion...28

5. Faith and Practice: Understanding the Qur'an's Message and its applications in our times...................................32

6. The Importance of Sunnah: The Practice of the Prophet Muhammad (pbuh)..35

7. The Five Pillars of Islam...37

8. Finding Your Place in the Ummah: The Collective Community of Muslims Worldwide...40

9. Islamic Law and the Modern World: Living in Accordance with the Qur'an..43

10. Mercy and Justice: The Qur'an's View of Human Rights..46

11. Living a Righteous Life: Living in Accordance with Islamic Values 49

12. Women in Islam: 21st Century Challenges 55

13. Fulfilling the Pursuit of Knowledge: Education in Islam 59

14. Following the Path of Modesty and Piety: Dress and Behaviour 64

15. Balance Between the Spiritual and The Mundane ..70

16. Handling difficult situations in life with the help of the Qur'an 73

17. Keeping You and Your Family Healthy 77

18. The Qur'an and Ecology: A Call for Stewardship of the Earth 80

19. Dealing with Stress and Anxiety: The Qur'an's Perspective 84

20. The Qur'an and Self-Improvement: Developing Mental and Spiritual Strength 87

21. Developing a Positive Attitude: Overcoming Negative Thinking 92

22. Tolerance and Respect: Interacting with People of Different Faiths 95

23. The Qur'an and Social Justice: Building a Better Society 99

24. The Qur'an and Politics: A Framework for a Just Society 102

25. Living with Patience and Resilience: How to Overcome Difficulties 105

26. Finding Peace and Contentment: The Qur'an's Perspective 108

27. Spiritual Growth: Awakening to the Qur'an's Wisdom 113

28. The Importance of Charity in Building A Just And Fair Society 116

29. The Qur'an and Science: Exploring the Wonders of the Universe 119

30. Serving Humanity: Working for Social Change 126

31. Forgiveness and Mercy: Embracing the Qur'an's Message 131

32. The Power of Prayer: Connecting with the Divine 135

33: Making the Most of Faith In The Modern World 138

34: Useful tips and concluding remarks 142

References 145

Glossary 146

Notes 156

Notes 157

Akhlaque Ahmed

A Note from The Author

This book is not intended for learned scholars of Islam, *per se*. It was my humble attempt to help lay people like me who are struggling to live in accordance with the Qur'an in the modern world, especially in the West. I believe that by understanding the teachings of the Qur'an and their relevance to life in the modern times, we can live better lives as believers. Through this book, I hope to provide readers with the tools they need to apply the teachings of the Qur'an to their lives and make the most of their faith.

The objectives of this book are to:

1. Provide an understanding of the teachings of the Qur'an and their relevance to life in the modern world.
2. Show how to practically apply the teachings of the Qur'an to everyday life.
3. Help readers develop a sense of balance between the spiritual and the mundane.
4. Show how to make the most of faith in the modern world.

This book is intended for anyone who is interested in learning how to apply the teachings of the Qur'an to their lives. It is particularly useful for Muslims who are struggling to balance their faith with the demands of the modern world. It is also suitable for non-Muslims who wish to gain an understanding of the Qur'an and its teachings.

I hope that by reading this book, readers will gain a better understanding of the teachings of the Qur'an and how to apply them to their lives in the modern world. I also hope that it will help readers develop a sense of balance and fulfillment in their lives and make the most of their faith. May Allah guide us all to the straight path and bless us with success on our journey.

Acknowledgement

I would like to express my heartfelt gratitude to my late father and spiritual teacher Shaykh Sultan Ahmed, for guiding me to the path of light and teaching me the importance of living by the Quran. His teachings and guidance have been an invaluable source of inspiration throughout my life.

My heartfelt thanks also go to all the Islamic scholars, teachers, and Shaykhs who have either taught me or shared their knowledge about the Quran and Islam with me for the past four decades. I especially recall Ustadh Abdullah Muhammad whose guidance has been invaluable in helping me understand the many teachings of the Quran, and I am deeply thankful for his unwavering support throughout this journey.

Finally, I would like to thank all my readers for their interest in this book. It is my sincere wish that this book will help the readers to understand and live by the teachings of the Quran.

Thank you all for your support and guidance.

Preface

This book provides a comprehensive guide to living a life based on the teachings of the Quran. It begins with an introduction to the Quran, outlining its core principles and values. Then, it delves into practical applications, such as how to properly connect to the Quran and use it as a source of guidance. Akhlaque also provides advice for how to best apply the Quran's teachings to modern life and how to use the Quran to develop meaningful relationships with others.

In addition, the book provides an insightful exploration of the spiritual aspects of living in accordance with the Quran. Akhlaque shares his personal experiences and reflections on how to cultivate an inner connection with the Quran and use it to find peace and contentment. He also offers guidance on how to live an ethical and moral life, as well as how to use the Quran to become a better person.

Readers may find some overlapping in some of the chapters and this is because all the chapters are written individually on a particular topic that could be read and appreciated stand-alone basis. Chapters are deliberately kept short so that readers are not bored and can finish a chapter in few minutes.

Whether you are looking to deepen your understanding of the Quran or are simply seeking a more meaningful life, How to Live by the Quran will provide you with the tools and insight for doing so. Akhlaque Ahmed's book is an invaluable guide to living a life of purpose and fulfillment.

Abdul Kadir Sughran

Introduction

The Qur'an is a timeless book of guidance that is applicable in any era and in any situation. It is the ultimate source of wisdom, morality and guidance for all mankind. To live by the Qur'an in modern times is not only possible, but a great blessing and opportunity. Living by the Qur'an will bring peace and contentment and open up the doors of success and prosperity.

The Qur'an provides us with clear guidance on every aspect of life, from the everyday details of our lives to our spiritual goals. We have been given clear instructions on how to live our lives according to the Qur'an, and if we follow these instructions, we can avoid many problems, and enjoy a life of prosperity and peace.

The first step in living by the Qur'an is to have faith in Allah and accept his teachings as the ultimate source of guidance. We must also have a commitment to implement the teachings of the Qur'an in our lives. We must strive to learn about the Qur'an and its teachings and practice its teachings in our daily lives.

The Qur'an teaches us to be honest, kind, and compassionate. We should strive to be honest and truthful in all our dealings, and to be kind and compassionate to those around us. We should also strive to maintain justice and fairness in all our dealings, and to treat everyone with respect and dignity.

The Qur'an also teaches us to be grateful for all that Allah has given us, and to use our blessings wisely and responsibly. We should not take Allah's blessings for granted but strive to use them to the best of our ability. We should also strive to be generous and kind to others, and to use our wealth and resources for the benefit of others.

The Qur'an also teaches us to be patient and steadfast in the face of adversity and difficulty. We should not give in to despair or give up hope in difficult times, but instead have faith that Allah will help us through our trials and tribulations. We should also strive to maintain a positive attitude and show patience and understanding towards others.

The Qur'an also teaches us to be humble and to be mindful of our actions. We should strive to avoid arrogance and pride, and instead strive to be humble and modest. We should also strive to be mindful of our actions, and to think before we act.

The Qur'an also teaches us to be thankful and to recognize our blessings. We should strive to show gratitude for all that Allah has given us, and to be thankful for all the blessings in our lives. We should also strive to recognize the blessings that Allah has bestowed upon us, and use them to the best of our ability.

The Qur'an also teaches us to be compassionate and forgiving. We should strive to forgive those who have wronged us, and to show mercy to those who need it. We should also strive to be compassionate and understanding towards others, and strive to make the world a better place.

Finally, the Qur'an teaches us to be content and satisfied with our lives. We should strive to be content with what we have, and to be satisfied with our lives. We

How to Live by The Qur'an

should also strive to be content with our circumstances, and to be grateful for all that we have.

Living by the Qur'an in modern times is not only possible but will bring great rewards and blessings. It is a great opportunity to learn and implement the teachings of the Qur'an in our lives, and to reap the rewards of a life of peace and contentment. The Qur'an is a timeless book of guidance that is applicable in any era and in any situation and living by the Qur'an in modern times will bring great rewards and blessings.

We pray that Allah grants us the guidance and strength to live our lives according to the teachings of the Qur'an, and to bring peace and contentment into our lives. May Allah guide us all in our journey and grant us the strength and courage to live by the Qur'an in modern times.

Verily, Allah knows best.

"And whoever fears Allah - He will make for him a way out. And will provide for him from where he does not expect. And whoever relies upon Allah - then He is sufficient for him. Indeed, Allah will accomplish His purpose. Allah has already set for everything a [decreed] extent." (Quran 65:2-3)

Akhlaque Ahmed

1. Introduction to the Quran, Its Core Principles, and Values

The Quran is a book of divine guidance that was revealed to the Prophet Muhammad (peace be upon him) over 1400 years ago. It is the central source of knowledge for the Islamic faith and serves as a guide for all of humanity. This book will explore the core principles and values of the Quran, with a focus on how to live one's life according to its teachings.

The Quran is the word of Allah, revealed to the Prophet Muhammad (peace be upon him) over the course of 23 years. It was revealed in Arabic and is preserved in its original form. The Quran is divided into 114 chapters, called surahs, and is composed of 6,236 verses.

The Quran was revealed as a book of guidance for all of humanity, and it is essential to understand its core principles and values in order to live a righteous and fulfilling life. The Quran is a source of wisdom, morality, and direction, and it provides guidance on how to live one's life in accordance with the will of Allah.

The Core Values of The Quran

The Quran is a source of guidance, and it outlines the core values that all believers should strive to uphold. These values are based on the fundamental principles of monotheism, justice, compassion, and mercy.

The Quran stresses the importance of monotheism, and it is the first and foremost principle of the Islamic faith. The Quran states: *"Say: He is Allah, the One!*

Allāh, the Eternal Refuge. He neither begets nor is born, Nor is there to Him any equivalent." (112:1-4). This verse emphasizes the oneness of Allah and the importance of worshiping Him alone.

The Quran also emphasizes the importance of justice and fairness. The Quran states: *"O you who have believed, be persistently standing firm in justice, witnesses for Allāh, even if it be against yourselves or parents and relatives. Whether one is rich or poor, Allāh is more worthy of both.1 So follow not [personal] inclination, lest you not be just. And if you distort [your testimony] or refuse [to give it], then indeed Allāh is ever, of what you do, Aware." (4:135).* This verse emphasizes the importance of standing up for justice, even if it is against one's own interests.

The Quran also emphasizes the importance of compassion and mercy. The Quran states: *"And do not let the hatred of a people for having obstructed you from al-Masjid al-Haram lead you to transgress. And cooperate in righteousness and piety, but do not cooperate in sin and aggression. And fear Allāh; indeed, Allāh is severe in penalty. (5:2).* This verse emphasizes the importance of being compassionate and merciful to fellow human beings and helping one another in righteousness and abstaining from helping one another in sin.

Finally, the Quran emphasizes the importance of patience and perseverance. The Quran states: *"Therefore be patient (O Muhammad), as were those of determination among the Messengers, and be in no haste about the (unbelievers). On the Day when they will see that (torment) with which they are promised (they will know)." (46:35)*. This verse emphasizes the importance of patience and perseverance, and that we do not need to be judgmental ourselves. Allah will ultimately reward those who are patient and steadfast in their faith.

The Quran as a Guide to life

The Quran is a guide to life, and it provides guidance on how to live a righteous and fulfilling life. The Quran outlines the core values that all believers should strive to uphold, and it provides guidance on how to live one's life according to these values.

The Quran provides guidance on how to interact with others in a respectful and kind manner. The Quran states: *"And speak kindly to people.." (2:83)*. This verse emphasizes the importance of treating others with kindness and respect.

The Quran also outlines the importance of maintaining good relationships with others. The Quran states: *"And hold firmly to the rope of Allah all together and do not become divided." (3:103)*. This verse emphasizes the importance of unity and community, and of maintaining good relationships with one's family, friends, and neighbours in a life centered around the 'rope of Allah', i.e., the Qur'an.

The Quran also outlines the importance of being mindful of one's actions and words. It states: *"And be moderate in your pace and lower your voice; indeed, the most disagreeable of sounds is the voice of donkeys." (31:19)*. This verse emphasizes the importance of being mindful of one's actions and words, and of avoiding loud and disruptive behaviour.

The Quran outlines the core values of monotheism, justice, compassion, and mercy, and it provides guidance on how to live one's life in accordance with these values. The Quran is a source of wisdom, morality, and direction, and it is essential for a Muslim to understand its core principles and values in order to live a righteous and fulfilling life.

2. Understanding the Qur'an in a Contemporary Context

The Qur'an is the primary source of Islamic guidance for Muslims. It is a book of divine revelation that is timeless and universal in its teachings. As such, its core messages and principles remain applicable to all times, places, and people. However, the world in which we live today is vastly different from the world in which the Qur'an was revealed. Therefore, it is important to understand how to interpret and apply the Qur'an in a modern context.

This chapter will discuss the importance of understanding the Qur'an in its contemporary context. It will explain how to interpret the Qur'an's teachings in light of modern developments, and how to apply them to our everyday lives. In addition, this chapter will provide an overview of the various ways in which the Qur'an can be studied in order to gain a deeper understanding of its wisdom and guidance.

The Qur'an: Guidance for Contemporary Times

The Qur'an is the primary source of guidance for Muslims. It is a book of divine revelation that contains timeless and universal messages. As such, its teachings remain applicable to all times and places. It is a source of guidance for Muslims in all aspects of life, from worship to social and economic matters.

However, it is important to note that the Qur'an was revealed in a context that is vastly different from the world we live in today. Therefore, it is important to understand how to interpret and apply the Qur'an's teachings in a modern context.

Interpreting the Qur'an in a Contemporary Context

In order to understand how to interpret the Qur'an in a contemporary context, it is important to recognize the difference between general principles and specific rulings. The Qur'an contains both general principles and specific rulings. General principles are timeless and universal, while specific rulings are context-specific.

For example, the Qur'an states that certain types of behaviour are prohibited, such as lying and stealing. These prohibitions are general principles that remain applicable in all contexts. On the other hand, the Qur'an also contains specific rulings, such as the prohibition of drinking alcohol, but it came into phases. The alcohol prohibition analogies are mentioned three times in three different chapters of Quran; a three-step prohibition which made it easier for those addicted to alcohol to stop it gradually. This ruling is specific to the context in which it was revealed and may not be applicable in our contexts, i.e. someone trying to take refuge under the verse that says *"O believers! Do not approach prayer while intoxicated until you are aware of what you say, nor in a state of 'full' impurity. (Quran, An-Nisa, 4:43).*

Therefore, it is important to recognize the difference between general principles and specific rulings when interpreting the Qur'an in a modern context. General principles remain applicable in all contexts, while specific rulings may need to be adapted to the modern context.

Applying the Qur'an in Everyday Life

How to Live by The Qur'an

The Qur'an contains timeless and universal principles that are applicable in all contexts. However, it is important to understand how to apply these principles to our everyday lives.

One way to do this is to reflect on the Qur'an's teachings and how they relate to our own lives. For example, the Qur'an emphasizes the importance of being truthful and honest in all aspects of life. This principle can be applied to our everyday lives by being honest and truthful in our interactions with others.

In addition, it is important to remember that the Qur'an is a book of guidance and wisdom. Therefore, it is important to seek guidance from the Qur'an in all aspects of life. This includes our everyday interactions with others, our decisions, and our actions. By doing so, we can gain a deeper understanding of the Qur'an's wisdom and guidance and use it to guide us in our lives today.

3. Connecting to the Qur'an and using it as a Source of Guidance

The Quran is the holy book of Islam, revealed to the Prophet Muhammad (peace be upon him) in the 7th century. It is the central religious text of Islam and is believed to be the word of Allah. As such, it is considered to be the ultimate source of guidance for Muslims. The Quran is divided into 114 chapters, known as Surahs, which are further divided into verses (Ayat). In its entirety, the Quran is a book of guidance, teaching us how to live our lives in accordance with the teachings of Islam.

As Muslims, we must strive to lead our lives in accordance with the teachings of the Quran and Sunnah. Connecting to the Quran is an important part of our journey as Muslims and is essential for leading a life of faith and righteousness. This chapter will provide tips and advice on how to properly connect to the Quran and use it as a source of guidance.

Understanding the Quran

The first step in connecting to the Quran is to understand its contents. This can be done by studying the Quran in its original Arabic language. Although many translations of the Quran are available in other languages, it is important to read and understand the Quran in its original Arabic language in order to gain the most benefit from it.

In order to understand the Quran, it is important to study the commentaries and interpretations of the Quran

How to Live by The Qur'an

by Islamic scholars. These commentaries and interpretations provide valuable insight into the meaning and context of the verses. Additionally, scholars can provide guidance and advice on how to apply the teachings of the Quran in our daily lives.

Reciting the Quran

The second step in connecting to the Quran is to recite it. Reciting the Quran is a form of dhikr (remembrance of Allah), which is highly recommended in Islam. It is believed that reciting the Quran brings peace and tranquility to the heart and can be a source of spiritual nourishment.

When reciting the Quran, it is important to ensure that one is reciting it properly and with accuracy. This can be done by studying the correct pronunciation of the Arabic language and taking classes on proper recitation if necessary. Additionally, it is important to recite the Quran with understanding and contemplation of its meaning.

Reflecting on the Quran

The third step in connecting to the Quran is to reflect on its verses. This can be done by reading the Quran and contemplating its verses. Reflecting on the Quran allows us to gain a deeper understanding of its teachings and apply them to our lives.

Additionally, reflecting on the Quran can help us to gain insight into our own lives and our own spiritual journey. Reflecting on the Quran can provide us with guidance and direction and can help us to make sense of difficult and trying times.

Living by the Quran

The fourth step in connecting to the Quran is to live by its teachings. This can be done by applying the teachings of the Quran in our daily lives. This includes striving to adhere to the five pillars of Islam, following the Sunnah (teachings) of the Prophet Muhammad (peace be upon him) and avoiding all forms of sin and evil.

It is important to remember that living by the Quran requires patience, dedication and perseverance. It is not something that can be done overnight, and it requires consistent effort and dedication for it to become part of our lives. Additionally, one should not be discouraged by any difficulties faced along the way, as these are part of the journey and can be used as an opportunity for growth.

Connecting to the Quran is an important step on the journey of faith for Muslims. It is the ultimate source of guidance and is the key to leading a life of faith and righteousness. Through understanding the Quran, reciting it properly, reflecting on its verses and living by its teachings, one can properly connect to the Quran and gain the most benefit from it. Additionally, one should always remember to seek guidance from Allah and the Prophet Muhammad (peace be upon him) in all matters. May Allah grant us the strength and guidance to properly connect to the Quran and use it as a source of guidance in our lives.

4. Living by the Qur'an: A Revelation of Mercy and Compassion

The Mercy and compassion are two of the foremost values upheld in the Quran and are essential for living a life of contentment and peace. The Quran teaches us that the mercy of God is infinite and that His compassion is boundless, and these teachings can be applied to our own lives if we take the time to understand them. In this chapter, we will explore how we can live our lives with the Quranic teachings of mercy and compassion.

The teachings of the Qur'an speak of mercy and compassion, and it is the foundation of Islam. Throughout the Qur'an, Allah speaks of humanity as His beloved vicegerent on earth and teaches us to be kind and merciful to one another. He emphasizes His mercy and compassion and shows us that His mercy surpasses His wrath.

Allah's Mercy in the Qur'an

The Qur'an is filled with verses and stories that demonstrate Allah's mercy and compassion for mankind. The very first verse of the Qur'an reads, "In the name of Allah, the Most Gracious, the Most Merciful" (Qur'an 1:1). In this verse, Allah identifies Himself as the Most Gracious and the Most Merciful, and this is repeated throughout the Qur'an. This verse is a reminder that Allah is the source of all mercy and compassion, and that He is always forgiving and merciful to us.

The Qur'an also speaks of Allah's mercy in many other verses. In Surah al-A'raf, Allah states, *"My mercy encompasses all things" (Qur'an 7:156)*. This verse shows us that Allah's mercy is infinite and that He is merciful to all of His creation. He is merciful not only to the believers, but also to the unbelievers. In Surah az-Zumar, Allah says, *"Say: O my Servants who have transgressed against their souls! Despair not of the Mercy of Allah: for Allah forgives all sins" (Qur'an 39:53)*. In Surah al-A'nam, Allah also says "Your Lord has decreed upon Himself mercy: that any of you who does wrong out of ignorance and then repents after that and corrects himself - indeed, He is Forgiving and Merciful." (Qur'an 6:54). These verses clearly show us that Allah is forgiving and merciful, even when we have done wrong.

Allah also speaks of His mercy and compassion in the stories of the prophets. In the story of Prophet Yusuf (Joseph), we see that despite the wrongs that he suffered, Yusuf was still merciful to his brothers. He was eventually reunited with his family and his brothers, and he had forgiven his brothers for their mistakes. This is a reminder that Allah is always merciful and compassionate, even when we have done wrong and how His chosen servants practiced it in their lives.

The Quran also speaks of the importance of being compassionate and merciful towards even to our enemies. Allah says, *"And if you punish (your enemy), then punish them with the like of that with which you were afflicted. But if you endure patiently, verily it is better for the patient." (Quran 16:126)*

This verse reminds us that we should strive to be patient and forgiving, even when faced with hostility. We should not seek revenge, but instead strive to be compassionate and merciful in our response. This is a reminder that Allah is the Most Merciful of all, and we should strive to imitate Him in our actions.

The Quran also speaks of the importance of being compassionate and merciful towards animals. Allah says, *"There is not an animal (that lives) on the earth, nor a being that flies on its wings, but (forms part of) communities like you. Nothing have we omitted from the Book, and they (all) shall be gathered to their Lord in the end." (Quran 6:38)*

This verse serves as a reminder that animals are part of the same community as us. We should strive to be merciful and compassionate towards them and treat them with the same respect and kindness that we would show to a fellow human being.

We must recognize that mercy and compassion are essential components of our lives, and that the Quran encourages us to practice them in all aspects of our lives. In the Quran, Allah states: *"And hasten to forgiveness from your Lord and a garden [i.e., Paradise] as wide as the heavens and earth, prepared for the righteous, who spend [in the cause of Allāh] during ease and hardship and who restrain anger and who pardon the people - and Allāh loves the doers of good; (3:133-134).* Pardoning the people means being 'Compassionate' to others.

These verses remind us that mercy and compassion are not only virtues to be practiced in our dealings with others but are also essential in our own internal lives, if we want to grace ourselves with the love of Allah and aspire to go to heaven. We must take care to show mercy and compassion to ourselves, to our thoughts, and to our emotions, so that we can be more understanding and accepting of our own mistakes and flaws.

Prophetic Examples of Mercy and Compassion

The teachings of the Qur'an are exemplified in the life of Prophet Muhammad (peace be upon him). He was known for his mercy and compassion for others, and he was a model for all of humanity. He was always forgiving and merciful, even to those who had wronged him. He was also known for his kind and gentle nature, and he was always willing to help those in need.

The Prophet Muhammad (peace be upon him) also taught us to be merciful to one another. He said, "Show mercy to those on earth, so that the One in Heaven will show mercy to you" (Hadith, Bukhari). This Hadith reminds us that we should be merciful and compassionate to one another, as Allah is merciful and compassionate to us.

In conclusion, as Muslims we should strive to be compassionate and merciful in our interactions with others, regardless of their social class or financial status. We should also strive to be kind and merciful to animals, and to be forgiving and patient with our enemies. By following these teachings, we can ensure that we are living our lives according to Allah's will and fulfilling our duty as believers.

5. Faith and Practice: Understanding the Qur'an's Message and its applications in our times

The Qur'an is the word of Allah, revealed to Prophet Muhammad (peace and blessings be upon him) over a period of 23 years. It is the living and unchanging source of guidance for all Muslims. The Qur'an is not a book of abstract philosophy, but a book of practical guidance for our lives. In this chapter, we will explore how to live according to the teachings of the Qur'an in modern times.

First, we will examine what faith and practice mean in the context of the Qur'an. We will then look at how to apply these concepts to our daily lives. Finally, we will discuss the importance of understanding the Qur'an's message and its application in our times.

Faith and Practice

Faith and practice are two important concepts in the Qur'an. Faith refers to our belief in Allah and His message. It is the foundation upon which all our actions should be based. The Qur'an states: *"Believers! Believe in Allah and His Messenger and in the Book He has revealed to His Messenger, and in the Book He revealed before. And whoever disbelieves in Allah, in His angels, in His Books, in His Messengers and in the Last Day, has indeed strayed far away." (Qur'an, 4:136).* This verse makes it clear that faith is not just about believing in Allah; it is also about believing in His Messenger and His book.

Practice is the practical application of our faith in our daily lives. It is the outward expression of our belief in Allah and His message. The Qur'an states: *"Believers! Obey Allah and obey the Messenger, and those from among you who are invested with authority; and then if you were to dispute among yourselves about anything refer it to Allah and the Messenger89 if you indeed believe in Allah and the Last Day; that is better and more commendable in the end"* (Qur'an, 4:59). This verse makes it clear that we must put our faith into practice and obey the commands of Allah and His Messenger.

Application of faith and practice

Once we have understood the concepts of faith and practice, we must begin to apply them to our daily lives. This means that we must strive to live according to the teachings of the Qur'an. This includes living with integrity, justice, and mercy, as well as following the Prophet's example.

We must also strive to be true to our faith by adhering to the five pillars of Islam and fulfilling our obligations as Muslims. This includes performing the five daily prayers, fasting during the month of Ramadan, giving charity, and making the pilgrimage to Mecca if we are able.

We must also strive to live in accordance with the Qur'an's teachings on social justice. This includes upholding the rights of all people, regardless of their religion or background. The Qur'an states: *"O you who believe, stand out firmly for justice, as witnesses to Allah, even though it be against yourselves, or your parents, or your kin, be he rich or poor, Allah is a Better Protector*

How to Live by The Qur'an

to both (than you)" (Qur'an, 4:135). This verse makes it clear that we must stand up for justice, even if it means going against our own interests.

Understanding the Qur'an's message and its application in our times

In order to live according to the teachings of the Qur'an, we must first understand its message and how it is applicable to our times. We must strive to understand the Qur'an's verses in their historical and cultural context in order to apply them to our lives and our times.

We must also strive to understand the Qur'an's teachings on social justice and how they can be applied to our times. We must strive to understand the Qur'an's teachings on gender equality, human rights, and economic justice, and how we can use these teachings to create a more just and equitable society.

Finally, we must strive to understand the Qur'an's guidance on how-to live in harmony with our families, friends, and neighbours. We must strive to understand the Qur'an's teachings on kindness, patience, and forgiveness, and how we can use them to create a more peaceful and harmonious society.

Living by the teachings of the Qur'an in modern times is not easy. It requires a deep understanding of its message and its application to our times. However, if we strive to understand the Qur'an's teachings and put them into practice in our daily lives, we can create a more just and peaceful society. We can also find guidance, peace, and happiness in our lives.

6. The Importance of Sunnah: The Practice of the Prophet Muhammad (pbuh)

In Islam, the practice of the Prophet Muhammad, known as the Sunnah, is an essential part of living a life of faith. The Sunnah is the record of the Prophet's sayings, deeds, and actions. It is seen as the practical example of how to live a life of faith and is used as a source of inspiration to Muslims.

The Quran mentions the Sunnah in many verses, emphasizing its importance and how it should be followed. In the Quran, Allah says: *"Indeed in the Messenger of Allah (Muhammad) you have a good example to follow for him who hopes for (the Meeting with) Allah and the Last Day and remembers Allah much" (Quran, 33:21).*

This verse clearly shows the importance of following the example of the Prophet Muhammad (pbuh) and how it is a source of guidance for Muslims. It also emphasizes the importance of having hope in Allah and being mindful of Him.

The Sunnah has been passed down through the generations and is seen by Muslims as a way to stay connected to the Prophet Muhammad (pbuh). It is a source of guidance, providing insight into how to live a life of faith and righteousness.

The Sunnah is applicable to all aspects of life, from worship to daily living. It is important for Muslims to understand and apply the Sunnah to their daily lives. For example, the Sunnah provides guidance on how to

How to Live by The Qur'an

perform the five pillars of Islam, such as prayer and fasting, and how to live according to the teachings of the Quran.

The Sunnah also provides guidance on how to interact with other people. It teaches us to be kind and compassionate to others, to be generous and charitable, and to be just and fair in our dealings.

The Sunnah also provides guidance on how to live a balanced life. It encourages Muslims to strive for excellence in all aspects of life, including their work, education, and leisure activities. It also emphasizes the importance of taking care of one's health, both physically and spiritually.

The Sunnah is an essential part of living a life of faith. It provides guidance on how to live a life of obedience to Allah and how to be a good and just person. It is a source of inspiration and a way to stay connected to the Prophet Muhammad (pbuh).

In our modern times, it is important for Muslims to remember the importance of the Sunnah and to strive to live according to its teachings. We must strive to follow the example of the Prophet Muhammad (pbuh) and use the Sunnah as a source of guidance and inspiration. We must also strive to be kind and compassionate to others and to live our lives in accordance with the teachings of the Quran. By doing so, we can remain connected to Allah and live a life of faith and righteousness.

7. The Five Pillars of Islam

The five pillars of Islam, i.e., Faith, Prayer, Pilgrimage, Fasting, and Charity are the five basic obligations of a Muslim in their faith. These pillars represent the core foundations of a Muslim's faith, and they are essential in order to live a life of faithfulness to the Qur'an. This chapter will discuss each of the five pillars in detail, while also exploring how to live by the Qur'an in the modern world.

The first pillar of Islam is faith. Faith is a fundamental part of the Muslim faith, and it is essential in order to live in accordance with the Qur'an. Faith is the belief in Allah and His Messengers, and it is the basis for all of the other pillars of Islam. The Qur'an states:

"The believers are only those who, when Allah is mentioned, their hearts become fearful, and when His verses are recited to them, it increases them in faith; and upon their Lord they rely." (Qur'an 8:2)

This verse emphasizes the importance of faith in the Muslim faith. Faith is essential for the believer to trust in Allah, and to live according to His commands.

The second pillar of Islam is obligatory prayer. Prayer is the foundation of a Muslim's daily life, and it is the most important part of a believer's faith. Prayer is a form of worship that is done five times a day, and it is essential in order to thank and seek guidance from Allah. The Qur'an states:

"And remember the favour of Allah upon you and His covenant with which He bound you when you

How to Live by The Qur'an

said: 'We hear and we obey.' And fear Allah, indeed, Allah is Knowing of that within the breasts." (Qur'an 5:7)

This verse emphasizes the importance of prayer in the Muslim faith as we made a covenant with Allah to 'obey Him'. Prayer is an act of obedience and submission to Allah, and it is essential in order to remain mindful of Him throughout the day.

The third pillar of Islam is fasting. Fasting is an obligation for all Muslims during the month of Ramadan, and it is a time for spiritual renewal and closeness to Allah. Fasting is an act of worship and devotion, and it is essential in order to gain a sense of humility and discipline. The Qur'an states:

"O you who have believed, decreed upon you is fasting as it was decreed upon those before you that you may become righteous." (Qur'an 2:183)

This verse emphasizes the importance of fasting in the Muslim faith. Fasting is an act of obedience and submission to Allah, and it is essential in order to gain a sense of humility and discipline.

The fourth pillar of Islam is pilgrimage. Pilgrimage is a once in a lifetime obligation for all able-bodied Muslims, and it is one of the most important aspects of the Muslim faith. Pilgrimage is a journey to the sacred city of Makkah, and it is a time for reflection, prayer, and spiritual renewal. The Qur'an states:

"And take a provision (with you) for the journey, but the best provision is At-Taqwa (piety, righteousness, etc.). So, fear Me, O men of understanding!" (Qur'an 2:197)

This verse emphasizes the importance of piety and righteousness in the Muslim faith. Pilgrimage is an opportunity for believers to renew their faith and connect with Allah, and to seek His guidance and mercy.

The fifth pillar of Islam is Zakat or charity. Charity is an essential part of the Muslim faith, and it is essential in order to help those in need. Charity is an act of kindness and generosity, and it is essential in order to show mercy and compassion towards others. The Qur'an states:

"And spend of that with which We have provided you before death comes to one of you and he says: 'My Lord, if only you would delay me for a short term so I would give charity and be among the righteous.'" (Qur'an 63:10)

This verse emphasizes the importance of charity in the Muslim faith. Charity is an act of kindness and generosity, and it is essential in order to show mercy and compassion towards others.

These five pillars are essential in order to live a life of faithfulness to the Qur'an. They represent the core foundations of a Muslim's faith, and they are essential in order to live in accordance with the Qur'an. By following these five pillars, Muslims can live a life of faithfulness to Allah, and to live in accordance with His guidance in the modern world.

8. Finding Your Place in the Ummah: The Collective Community of Muslims Worldwide

In the Qur'an, Allah has not only given us guidance on how to live our individual lives, but He has also supplied us with the tools to live as a collective Ummah (community). This guidance has been provided in the form of teachings and examples from the Prophet Muhammad (peace be upon him). In this chapter, we will explore how we can apply these teachings and examples to our lives in the modern world.

In the Qur'an, Allah states: *"And hold fast, all together, by the rope of Allah (stretches out for you) and be not divided among yourselves"* (Surah Al-Imran 3:103). Most of the scholars defined *the rope of Allah* as the Quran itself. This verse is a reminder to us that we should hold fast to the rope of Allah and remain united as a single body. We should not be divided by our differences in race, colour, language, culture, or any other factor. All Muslims are members of one Ummah and should strive to live in harmony and unity.

The concept of Ummah is closely linked to the notion of universal brotherhood and sisterhood of the believers. Allah states in the Qur'an: *"And among His Signs is this, that He created for you mates from among yourselves, that ye may dwell in tranquility with them, and He has put love and mercy between your (hearts): Verily in that are Signs for those who reflect"* (Surah Ar-Rum 30:21). This verse reminds us that we should love and care for one another as members of the Ummah.

We should strive to be compassionate and understanding towards our fellow believers, regardless of any differences we may have.

The Prophet Muhammad (peace be upon him) also emphasized the importance of unity within the Ummah. He said: "The similitude of believers in regard to mutual love, affection, and fellow-feeling is that of one body; when any limb of it aches, the whole-body aches, because of sleeplessness and fever" (Bukhari, Muslim). This hadith shows us the importance of unity within the Ummah and how we should strive to look out for each other and be supportive of one another.

The Ummah is not just limited to Muslims living in our own localities or countries. We are a global Ummah, and our boundaries are not limited by physical borders or nationalities. Allah states in the Qur'an: *"Verily, the Muslims are a single brotherhood" (Surah Al-Hujurat 49:10)*. This verse reminds us that we are all brothers and sisters in faith, regardless of where we may live. We should strive to treat each other with respect, love, and compassion, and to support each other in times of difficulty.

We should also strive to work together to serve the Ummah in any way we can. The Prophet Muhammad (peace be upon him) said: "The believers in their mutual kindness, compassion and sympathy are just like one body. When any part of the body suffers, the whole body feels pain" (Bukhari, Muslim). This hadith shows us the importance of working together to serve the Ummah. We should strive to help each other and work together to improve the lives of others.

In the modern world, there are many challenges that the Ummah is facing. One of the worst things that has plagued the Muslim Ummah is the geographical and linguistic nationalism. We need to come together and work together to address these challenges. We should strive to support each other, to speak up for those who cannot speak for themselves, and to defend the rights of our fellow Muslims who are suffering injustice. We should not be divided by our differences but should strive to work together to build a better future for our Ummah.

In conclusion, we, as Muslims, are all members of one global Ummah. We should strive to unite with each other and to uphold the principles of brotherhood and sisterhood. We should strive to help and support our fellow Muslims, to speak up for those who cannot speak for themselves, and to work together to serve the Ummah. By doing this, we can ensure that our Ummah remains strong and united.

9. Islamic Law and the Modern World: Living in Accordance with the Qur'an

The Qur'an is a timeless book, written for all of humanity throughout the ages. It is a book of guidance for believers and a source of wisdom for all people. As such, it is important to look at how the Qur'an can be applied to everyday life in the modern world. In this chapter we will discuss Islamic law and how it relates to the modern world.

To understand the impact of Islamic law on the modern world, it is important to first understand what Islamic law is and how it is derived from the Qur'an. Islamic law is based on the teachings of the Qur'an and the Sunnah, or practice, of the Prophet Muhammad (peace be upon him). It is derived from the four main sources of Islamic jurisprudence, which are the Qur'an, Sunnah, the consensus of scholars, and analogical reasoning.

The Qur'an is the primary source of Islamic law. It contains the laws and principles that govern the lives of Muslims. The Qur'an is divided into verses, or Ayat, which are the basis for Islamic law. It is believed that Allah revealed the Qur'an to the Prophet Muhammad (peace be upon him) as guidance for humanity. The Qur'an provides a comprehensive system of law, covering all aspects of life, from the spiritual to the mundane.

The Sunnah is the practice of the Prophet Muhammad (peace be upon him). It includes his sayings, actions, and approval of certain actions. The Sunnah is used to explain and provide further guidance on the teachings of the Qur'an. For example, the Prophet Muhammad (peace be upon him) gave detailed instructions on how to perform the Hajj (pilgrimage to Mecca).

The consensus of scholars is an important source of Islamic law. It is based on the collective wisdom of Islamic scholars who have studied and debated on the Qur'an and the Sunnah. The scholars use the Qur'an and Sunnah to reach a consensus on issues of Islamic law.

Analogical reasoning is the fourth source of Islamic jurisprudence. It is based on the concept of qiyas, which means to make an analogy between two things. It is used to derive rules from the Qur'an and Sunnah that are not explicitly mentioned.

The Qur'an and Sunnah provide guidance on all aspects of life, from worship and morality to business and marriage. Islamic law covers a wide range of topics, such as marriage, divorce, inheritance, contracts, and criminal justice. Islamic law also provides guidance on social issues, such as education, health, and welfare.

The Qur'an and Sunnah provide specific guidance on how to live a life of faith and obedience to Allah. They provide guidance on how to be a good citizen and how to treat others with kindness and respect. The Qur'an and Sunnah also provide guidance on how to live in harmony with the Nature and be mindful of the environment.

Islamic law is applicable to all Muslims, regardless of where they live and what their social and economic circumstances are. The principles of Islamic law are universal and apply to all Muslims, regardless of their location or background.

Islamic law is also flexible and able to adapt to the changing needs of society. The principles of Islamic law are timeless and are applicable to all times and places. Islamic law is not static but is able to evolve to meet the changing needs of society.

In the modern world, Islamic law is often misunderstood and misinterpreted. Many people view Islamic law as outdated and oppressive. However, this is not the case. Islamic law provides guidance on how to live a life of faith and obedience to Allah. It is a comprehensive system of law that applies to all aspects of life, from the spiritual to the mundane.

Islamic law is relevant to the modern world because it provides guidance on how to live a life of faith and obedience to Allah. It is a comprehensive system of law that is applicable to all times and places. It is flexible and able to adapt to the changing needs of society. Islamic law is not outdated or oppressive, but instead provides guidance on how to live a life of faith and obedience to Allah.

In conclusion, Islamic law is a comprehensive system of law that applies to all aspects of life. It is derived from the four main sources of Islamic jurisprudence, which are the Qur'an, Sunnah, the consensus of scholars, and analogical reasoning. Islamic law is applicable to all Muslims, regardless of their location or background. It is flexible and able to adapt to the changing needs of society. Islamic law provides guidance on how to live a life of faith and obedience to Allah. It is relevant to the modern world and provides guidance on how to live a life of faith and obedience to Allah.

10. Mercy and Justice: The Qur'an's View of Human Rights

The Qur'an, the holy book of Islam, speaks strongly against injustice and encourages its followers to practice mercy and justice in all aspects of life. In particular, the Qur'an emphasizes the importance of respecting the rights of all human beings and treating them with dignity and fairness. In the Qur'an, Allah commands human beings to be just and merciful in all of their dealings with one another.

The Qur'an is clear in its condemnation of injustice and its demand for justice. In one verse, Allah says, *"O you who have faith! Be upholders of justice, bearing witness for Allah alone, even if it be against yourselves or parents and relatives. Whether one is rich or poor, Allah is more worthy of both. So do not follow your desires, lest you swerve from justice; for if you distort or neglect justice, verily Allah is well aware of what you do" (4:135)*. This verse makes it clear that justice is the responsibility of all believers, regardless of their circumstances or relationships.

The Qur'an also emphasizes the importance of mercy, which it defines as being generous, kind and forgiving. In one verse, Allah says, *"And let not your hand be tied (in generosity) to your neck, nor stretch it forth to its utmost reach, so that you become blameworthy and destitute" (17:29)*. This verse makes it clear that believers should not be miserly with their

How to Live by The Qur'an

resources but should instead be generous and compassionate.

In addition to justice and mercy, the Qur'an also speaks of the importance of equality and fairness. In one verse, Allah says, *"O mankind! We have created you from a single (pair) of a male and a female, and made you into nations and tribes, that you may know each other (not that you may despise each other)" (49:13)*. This verse makes it clear that all human beings are equal and should be treated with fairness and respect.

The Qur'an also speaks of the importance of human dignity and freedom. In one verse, Allah says, *"He is the One Who created you from a single soul, then from it made its spouse so he may find comfort in her. After he had been united with her, she carried a light burden that developed gradually. When it grew heavy, they prayed to Allah, their Lord, "If you grant us good offspring, we will certainly be grateful" (7:189)*. This verse makes it clear that all human beings have the right to dignity and freedom and should be treated with kindness and respect.

The Qur'an also speaks of the importance of human rights, such as the right to life, liberty, and the pursuit of happiness. In one verse, Allah says, *"And whosoever kills a believer intentionally, his recompense is Hell, to abide therein; and the wrath and the curse of Allah are upon him, and a dreadful penalty is prepared for him" (4:93)*. This verse makes it clear that believers should respect the life and liberty of all human beings.

Finally, the Qur'an speaks of the importance of protecting the environment and caring for all of Allah's creatures. In one verse, Allah says, *"And there is not a single creature on earth but its provision is due from Allah" (11:6)*. This verse makes it clear that believers should care for the environment and all living creatures and should not waste or destroy resources out of greed or selfishness.

In conclusion, the Qur'an speaks strongly against injustice and encourages its followers to practice mercy and justice in all aspects of life. The Qur'an emphasizes the importance of respecting the rights of all human beings and treating them with dignity and fairness. It also speaks of the importance of protecting the environment and caring for all of Allah's creatures. By following the teachings of the Qur'an, believers can ensure that their dealings with others are fair and just, and that their actions are in accordance with Allah's will.

11. Living a Righteous Life: Living in Accordance with Islamic Values

Living a righteous life is one of the most important aspects of following the teachings of the Qur'an in modern times. The Qur'an provides us with clear guidance on how to live our lives in accordance with Islamic values and principles. We will explore the various aspects of this in this chapter.

1. Obey Allah and His Messenger:

The first and most important way to live a righteous life in accordance with Islamic values is to obey Allah and His messenger. The Qur'an makes it very clear that we should obey Allah and His messenger:

"O you who have believed, obey Allah and obey the Messenger and those in authority among you. And if you disagree over anything, refer it to Allah and the Messenger, if you should believe in Allah and the Last Day. That is the best [way] and best in result." (Qur'an 4:59)

This verse makes it very clear that if we want to live a righteous life, we must obey Allah and His messenger. This means that we must follow the teachings of the Qur'an and the teachings of the Prophet Muhammad (peace be upon him). We must also obey those in authority over us, as long as their commands do not contradict the teachings of the Qur'an or the teachings of the Prophet Muhammad (peace be upon him).

2. Be Just and Righteous:

The Qur'an also tells us to be just and righteous in our dealings with others:

"O you who have believed, be persistently standing firm in justice, witnesses for Allah, even if it be against yourselves or parents and relatives. Whether one is rich or poor, Allah is more worthy of both. So follow not [personal] inclination, lest you not be just. And if you distort [your testimony] or refuse [to give it], then indeed Allah is ever, with what you do, Acquainted." (Qur'an 4:135)

This verse makes it very clear that we should always strive to be just and righteous in our dealings with others. We should not let our personal biases or desires cloud our judgement. We should always strive to be fair and just in all our dealings, whether it be with our family, friends, or acquaintances.

3. Honour Promises and Contracts:

The Qur'an also tells us to honour our promises and contracts:

"And fulfill the covenant of Allah when you have taken it, [O believers], and do not break oaths after their confirmation while you have made Allah, over you, a witness. Indeed, Allah knows what you do." (Qur'an 16:91)

This verse makes it very clear that we should always strive to honour our promises and contracts. This means that we should not break our promises or breach our contracts. We should always strive to keep our word and be honest in our dealings.

4. Be Kind and Courteous:

The Qur'an also tells us to be kind and courteous to others:

"And not equal are the good deed and the bad. Repel [evil] by that [deed] which is better; and thereupon the one whom between you and him is enmity [will become] as though he was a devoted friend." (Qur'an 41:34)

This verse makes it very clear that we should always strive to be kind and courteous to others, even if they are our enemies. We should always strive to do good deeds, even if they are met with hostility. We should not retaliate with bad deeds, but instead, strive to do good deeds and be kind to others, regardless of their attitude towards us.

5. Do Not Bear False Witness:

Making false statement or bearing false witness is a sin before Allah. The Qur'an also tells us not to bear false witness:

and do not deprive people of what is rightfully theirs; and do not act wickedly on earth by spreading corruption/mischief. [Qur'an 26:183]

In another place, the Quran says:

"O you who have believed, be persistently standing firm for Allah, witnesses in justice, and do not let the hatred of a people prevent you from being just. Be just; that is nearer to righteousness. And fear Allah; indeed, Allah is Acquainted with what you do." (Qur'an 5:8)

These verses make it very clear that we should not bear false witness. We should always strive to be truthful in our speech and honest in our dealings. We should not let our hatred for someone prevent us from being just and truthful.

6. Show Compassion and Mercy:

The Qur'an also tells us to show compassion and mercy to others:

"And be merciful and compassionate to one another." (Qur'an 24:22)

This verse makes it very clear that we should always strive to be compassionate and merciful to others. We should not be quick to judge or be harsh in our dealings with others. We should always strive to show kindness, compassion, and mercy to those around us.

7. Spend in the Way of Allah:

The Qur'an also tells us to spend in the way of Allah:

"And spend [in the way of Allah] from what We have provided you before death approaches one of you and he says, 'My Lord, if only You would delay me for a brief term so I would give charity and be among the righteous.'" (Qur'an 63:10)

This verse makes it very clear that we should strive to spend in the way of Allah. This means that we should give charity, help those in need, and strive to do good deeds. We should not be miserly with our wealth and resources, but rather use them to do good.

8. Put Your Trust in Allah:

The Qur'an also tells us to put our trust in Allah:

"And whoever relies upon Allah - then He is sufficient for him." (Qur'an 65:3)

This verse makes it very clear that we should always strive to put our trust in Allah. We should not worry about the things that are beyond our control, but rather trust that Allah will take care of us. We should have faith in Allah's plans and trust that He will provide for us.

9. Be Patient and Steadfast:

The Qur'an also tells us to be patient and steadfast:

"O you who have believed, seek help through patience and prayer. Indeed, Allah is with the patient." (Qur'an 2:153)

This verse makes it very clear that we should strive to be patient and steadfast in our endeavors. We should not give up when faced with difficulties, but rather persevere and be steadfast in our faith. We should not be quick to despair, but rather trust in Allah and be patient in our trials.

10. Seek Knowledge and Reflection:

The Qur'an also tells us to seek knowledge and reflection:

"Say, 'Are those who know equal to those who do not know?' Only they will remember [who are] people of understanding." (Qur'an 39:9)

This verse makes it very clear that we should always strive to seek knowledge and reflect on our lives. We should not be content with what we know, but rather strive to learn more and grow in our faith. We should use our knowledge to reflect on our lives and strive to become better Muslims.

In conclusion, living a righteous life in accordance with Islamic values is essential for those who want to follow the teachings of the Qur'an in modern times. We must obey Allah and His messenger, be just and righteous, honour our promises and contracts, be kind and courteous, do not bear false witness, show compassion and mercy, spend in the way of Allah, put our trust in Allah, be patient and steadfast, and seek knowledge and reflection. By following these principles, we can strive to live a life in accordance with Islamic values and principles.

12. Women in Islam: 21st Century Challenges

The role of women in Islam is a controversial and often misunderstood subject. It has been the subject of much debate and discussion, both in the Muslim world and in the West. There are many opinions and interpretations of the Quranic verses pertaining to the rights and roles of women in Islam. This chapter will provide a brief overview of the various interpretations and discuss some of the challenges faced by women in the modern world.

The Qur'an and Women:

The Qur'an is a book that speaks to both men and women and provides them with guidance on how to live their lives in accordance with the will of Allah. The Qur'an is clear in its message that both men and women are equal in the eyes of Allah and should be treated as such.

In the Qur'an, it is stated that men and women are created from the same soul and are thus equal in the sight of Allah (4:1). The Qur'an also makes it clear that both men and women have responsibilities and rights in the eyes of Allah (2:228). Furthermore, the Qur'an makes it clear that men and women have similar responsibilities and rights when it comes to matters of faith, marriage, divorce, and inheritance (4:19, 4:34, 4:176).

In addition to these rights and responsibilities, the Qur'an also outlines the roles of men and women in society. Men are expected to be the primary breadwinners, protectors, and providers for their families. Women are expected to be caretakers, nurturers, and educators in the home. The Qur'an also outlines the importance of respecting and honouring one another, regardless of gender (4:19).

The traditional view of women in Islam:

The traditional view of women in Islam is one of respect and honour. Women are seen as being of equal value to men and are expected to fulfill the roles outlined in the Qur'an. In traditional Islamic societies, women are expected to dress modestly and to behave in a respectful manner at all times. They are expected to obey their husbands and to remain chaste. They are also expected to take care of the home and the children.

The Quran outlines the rights of women in a number of ways, including their right to education, their rights within marriage, and even the rights of widows and orphans. Education is a fundamental right for all Muslims, regardless of gender. Women are allowed to pursue higher education and are even encouraged to do so. The Quran also grants women the right to choose their own spouse and to enter into marriages of their own free will.

In terms of marriage, the Quran outlines a number of rights that women have. This includes the right to maintain their own independent financial assets, the right to receive a dowry before the consummation of the marriage, and the right to receive alimony in the event of a divorce. The Quran also stresses the importance of mutual respect and kindness within a marriage and

How to Live by The Qur'an

encourages both men and women to treat each other fairly and with respect.

The Quran also outlines the rights of widows and orphans. Widows are allowed to inherit from their deceased spouse and are also entitled to receive financial support from their family if needed. Orphans are given special protection under the law and are provided with food, shelter, and clothing.

Despite the traditional view of women in Islam, it is important to note that the Qur'an does not prescribe any particular type of behaviour or lifestyle for women. Instead, it urges people to think for themselves and to make decisions based on what they believe is right. Furthermore, the Qur'an emphasizes that both men and women should strive to be their best selves, and to work together to create a better society.

21st century challenges

In the modern world, women face a variety of challenges that were not as prevalent in traditional Islamic societies as they are today. One of the most significant challenges is the issue of gender inequality. In many parts of the world, women are still not afforded the same rights and privileges as men and are often excluded from decision making processes. Additionally, in many countries, women are not given the same access to education and employment opportunities as men.

Another challenge faced by women in the modern world is the issue of violence and harassment. Despite the Quranic emphasis on respect for women, many women around the world are still victims of physical, emotional, and psychological abuse. It is also important to note that these challenges are not confined to Muslim countries, as women in the West also face many of the same issues.

In conclusion, it is clear that the role of women in Islam is complex and multi-faceted. The Qur'an outlines the rights and responsibilities of both men and women and encourages both genders to strive for their best selves. However, in the modern world, women are still facing a variety of challenges that need to be addressed. It is important that we continue to strive for gender equality and respect for all individuals, regardless of gender. Only then will we be able to create a society where both men and women can live and work together in harmony.

13. Fulfilling the Pursuit of Knowledge: Education in Islam

In the Qur'an, Allah has emphasized the importance of attaining knowledge and educating oneself. In fact, the first revealed word of the Quran was 'Iqra' which means 'READ'. Allah says in the Qur'an in Surah Al-Baqarah:

"And say, 'My Lord, increase me in knowledge" (20:114).

The pursuit of knowledge is one of the essential Islamic values that should be sought and encouraged. Education is a way of learning, understanding, and acquiring knowledge, skills, and values. It is a process of developing the intellect, character, and moral qualities of an individual.

In Islam, education is a moral responsibility for every Muslim, regardless of gender, age, or social status. It is considered a form of worship and a key to success in both the worldly life and the Hereafter. In this chapter, we will discuss the importance of education in Islam, the importance of seeking knowledge, Islamic educational methods, and the importance of educating our children in the Qur'anic teachings.

I. The Importance of Education in Islam

The importance of education in Islam is highlighted in numerous verses of the Qur'an. Allah says in the Quran *"There is no god but He: That is the witness of Allah, His angels, and those endued with knowledge, standing firm on justice. There is no god but He, the Exalted in Power, the Wise" [Quran, 3:18].*

In this verse, *and those endued with knowledge* refers to the people who actively pursue knowledge and it is expected that this kind of people will eventually know about one true Allah. Also, for us, we cannot just assume that we believe in the Oneness of Allah, we must actively learn and obtain knowledge to truly understand the greatness and oneness of Allah – which will help us stand firm on the path of righteousness.

In surah Tawba Allah says:

"It is not right for all the believers to go out [to battle] together: out of each community, a group should go out to gain understanding of the religion, so that they can teach their people when they return and so that they can guard themselves against evil.(9:122)

This verse emphasizes the importance of gaining knowledge and wisdom. Additionally, Allah says in Surah Nisa:

Allah has revealed to you the Book and wisdom and has taught you that which you did not know. And ever has the favor of Allah upon you been great." (4:113).

This verse highlights the importance of acquiring knowledge and that knowledge is a great favour from the creator.

Education is not only important for personal growth and development but also for the development of society as a whole. Education is a way to acquire knowledge and skills that are necessary to be successful in various areas of life. Education can also help people become more productive, successful, and better citizens of the society.

In Islam, education is a moral responsibility that should not be taken lightly. Muslims must strive to acquire knowledge and wisdom in order to better understand the teachings of Islam and to be able to practice it in their daily lives.

II. The Importance of Seeking Knowledge

The importance of seeking knowledge is highlighted in many verses of the Qur'an. Allah says in Surah Al-Muzzammil:

"And say, 'My Lord, increase me in knowledge'" (20:114).

This verse emphasizes the importance of seeking knowledge, as it is a way to increase one's understanding of the teachings of the Qur'an.

Additionally, Allah says in Surah An-Ankabut:

"And those who strive for Us – We will surely guide them to Our ways" (29:69).

This verse highlights the importance of striving to the cause of Allah and one's striving and efforts to acquire knowledge and wisdom is not excluded from striving to the cause of Allah.

Seeking knowledge is also a way to stay connected to Allah. The Quran urges the mankind to think, ponder, reflect and acquire knowledge that would bring them closer to God and his creation. The Quran uses repetition to embed certain key concepts in the consciousness of its listeners. Allah (God) and Rab (the Sustainer) are repeated 2,800 and 950 times, respectively, in the sacred text; Ilm (knowledge) comes third with 750 mentions.

The mentioning of Ilm (knowledge) for 750 times in the Quran highlights the importance of seeking knowledge, as it is a way to stay connected to Allah and to increase in guidance.

III. Islamic Educational Methods

In Islam, education is a holistic process that encompasses both knowledge and character building. The goal of Islamic education is to inculcate Islamic values and to develop an individual's moral character.

Islamic education emphasizes the importance of both formal and informal education. Formal education is important for gaining knowledge and skills, while informal education is important for developing moral character.

The Qur'an and the Sunnah of the Prophet Muhammad (PBUH) are the primary sources of Islamic education. Islamic educational methods include memorization of the Qur'an, studying the translation and interpretation of the Qur'an, and learning Hadith and Fiqh. Additionally, Islamic education also includes study of the sciences and the arts.

IV. Educating Our Children in Qur'anic Teachings

It is important to educate our children in the Qur'anic teachings and to instill in them the values and morals of Islam.

In the Qur'an, Allah says in Surah Al-Talaq:

"O you who have believed, protect yourselves and your families from a Fire whose fuel is people and stones" (66:6).

How to Live by The Qur'an

This verse emphasizes the importance of protecting our families and children from hellfire. The best way to protect someone from danger is to educate them about the danger and teach the skills and tools so that they can protect themselves. Educating our children is a means that would allow them to lead a successful life in this world and the Hereafter.

The Prophet Muhammad (PBUH) said: "The best of you are those who are best to their families." (Bukhari).

This Hadith emphasizes the importance of being a role model in front of our children and as a role model we need to educate our children in the teachings of the Qur'an and instilling in them the values of Islam.

In conclusion, education is an important Islamic value that should be pursued and encouraged. The Qur'an and the Sunnah of the Prophet Muhammad (PBUH) are the primary sources of Islamic education. It is important to educate our children in the Qur'anic teachings and to instill in them the values and morals of Islam. Education is a way to acquire knowledge and skills that are necessary to be successful in various areas of life. Education is also a way to stay connected to Allah and to increase in guidance.

14. Following the Path of Modesty and Piety: Dress and Behaviour

Islam is a religion of modesty and purity and one of the ways to show this is through our dress and behaviour. The Qur'an encourages us to dress and behave modestly and to be conscious of our behaviour. This chapter focuses on the importance of modesty and piety in the way we dress and behave in the modern times.

The Qur'an has clear guidelines on how Muslims should dress and behave. The Qur'an tells us that:

"Say to the believing men that they should lower their gaze and guard their modesty; that will make for greater purity for them; and Allah is well acquainted with all that they do" (Quran 24:30).

The Prophet Muhammad (peace be upon him) also taught us that:

"The most perfect of believers in faith is he who is best in manners and kindest to his family" (Hadith, Bukhari).

The Qur'an also encourages us to be mindful of our behaviour and to be conscious of the words that we use. The Qur'an says:

"And speak to people good [words] and establish prayer and give zakah" (Quran 2:83).

It is clear from these verses from the Qur'an that Muslims should behave with modesty and piety.

The Qur'an also states that:

"And tell the believing women to lower their gaze, and be modest, and to display of their adornment

only that which is apparent, and to draw their veils over their bosoms, and not to reveal their adornment save to their own husbands" (Quran 24:31).

This verse from the Qur'an tells us that women should lower their gaze, be modest, and not to reveal their adornment to anyone other than their own husbands. This means that women should cover their hair, body and neck, and should not wear revealing clothing.

The Qur'an also states that:

"O children of Adam, We have bestowed upon you clothing to cover your shame, and as adornment. But the clothing of righteousness - that is best. That is from the signs of Allah that perhaps they will remember" (Quran 7:26).

This verse from the Qur'an tells us that all people should wear clothing that is modest, appropriate, and in line with the teachings of the Qur'an, bearing in mind that the best clothing is the clothing of *righteousness or* Taqwa.

It is important to note that these guidelines from the Qur'an and hadith are not only about dressing modestly but also about protecting our privacy and not exposing ourselves to others. The Qur'an states that:

"Do not display yourselves like that of the times of ignorance" (Quran 33:33).

This verse from the Qur'an tells us that we should not display ourselves in a manner that is inappropriate, offensive, or disrespectful.

When it comes to our behaviour, the Qur'an encourages us to be mindful of our words and actions. The Qur'an states that:

"And let not the hatred of a people prevent you from being just. Be just; that is nearer to piety" (Quran 5:8).

This verse from the Qur'an tells us that we should not let hatred lead us to behave in an unjust manner. We should be just and kind in all our dealings with others and not let our emotions get the best of us.

The Qur'an also states that:

"And be not like those who come out of their homes boastfully and to be seen of men, and debar (men) from the way of Allah" (Quran 8:47).

This verse from the Qur'an tells us that we should not behave in a way that is boastful or ostentatious. We should be humble and not look down on others.

The Prophet Muhammad (peace be upon him) also taught us about being mindful of our behaviour. He said:

"The most perfect of believers in faith is he who is best in manners and kindest to his family" (Hadith, Bukhari).

This hadith tells us that we should be kind and courteous to our family and friends and treat them with respect and kindness.

Islamic Dress Code

The Islamic dress code is a set of guidelines which dictate the type of clothing to be worn by adherents of the Islamic faith. It is a religious requirement that all Muslims adhere to, and it is an important part of their faith. The Islamic dress code has been established by

Islamic scholars and is based on the teachings of the Qur'an and the Hadith.

The Islamic dress code is based on modesty and the purpose of the dress code is to protect the modesty and honor of the believer. The Qur'an states: "Tell the believing men to reduce [some] of their vision and guard their private parts. That is purer for them. Indeed, Allah is Acquainted with what they do." (Qur'an, 24:30). This verse is interpreted as a commandment to cover the body and to wear loose fitting clothing.

The Islamic dress code is different for men and women. Men are required to cover the body from the navel to the knees. Women are required to cover the entire body with the exception of the face and hands. Both genders must wear clothing that is not see-through or transparent.

Some may argue that the Islamic dress code for women is stricter than that of men. Women are required to wear a hijab, which is a covering for the head and chest. The hijab is usually a scarf that is worn over the head and under the chin. It is also important for women to wear loose fitting clothing that does not reveal the shape of the body.

In addition to the Islamic dress code, there are other rules which govern the behavior of Muslims. Muslims are expected to abstain from any type of public display of affection, including hand holding and hugging. They are also expected to avoid wearing revealing clothing such as short skirts and tight clothing.

The Islamic dress code is an important part of the Islamic faith, and it is important for Muslims to adhere to these guidelines. It is important to remember that the Islamic dress code is not only a matter of faith but also a way to protect the modesty and honor of the believer. As Muslim women, it is important to remember that the Islamic dress code is not just about covering the body, but also about respecting the beliefs of others.

The Qur'an and hadith provide guidance and examples on how to adhere to the Islamic dress code. The hadith of the Prophet Muhammad (peace be upon him) states: "The best garment of the believer is the garment of modesty." (Hadith, Sahih Muslim). This hadith encourages modesty and discourages the wearing of revealing clothing.

The Qur'an also states: "O Prophet, tell your wives and your daughters and the women of the believers to bring down over themselves [part] of their outer garments. That is more suitable that they will be known and not be abused." (Qur'an, 33:59). This verse is interpreted as a commandment for women to cover their bodies and is a reminder to maintain modesty.

The Islamic dress code is an important part of the faith and should be respected. It is important to remember that the dress code is not only a matter of faith, but also a way to protect the modesty and honor of the believer. The Qur'an and hadith provide guidance and examples on how to adhere to the Islamic dress code and Muslims should strive to follow these guidelines.

In conclusion, it is important for Muslims to dress and behave with modesty and piety in the modern times. The Qur'an and hadith provide us with clear guidelines on how to dress and behave modestly and respectfully.

How to Live by The Qur'an

We should be mindful of our words and actions and strive to be just and kind to others. By following these guidelines, we can embody the teachings of the Qur'an and be an example of modesty and piety for others.

15. Balance Between the Spiritual and The Mundane

In modern times, the way of living based on the Qur'an can be a challenge. It is easy to become overwhelmed by the fast-paced life of modern society and lose sight of the spiritual aspects of life that the Qur'an offers. This chapter is designed to help readers develop a sense of balance between the spiritual and the mundane so that they can lead a life of purpose and fulfillment.

Living with a sense of balance between the spiritual and the mundane is not an easy task, but it is possible. The key is to ensure that both aspects of life are taken care of with equal importance and dedication. This can be achieved by following the teachings of the Qur'an and seeking guidance from Allah. As Allah says in the Qur'an: *"Those who believe and do righteous deeds, they are the best of creatures" (Surah Al-Bayyinah: 98:7).*

Living a life of balance

Living a life of balance between the spiritual and the mundane is essential for leading a fulfilling life. In order to achieve this balance, it is essential to understand the importance of both aspects of life. The spiritual aspect of life helps us to connect with Allah and strengthen our faith, while the mundane aspect of life helps us to fulfill our worldly obligations and provide for our needs. Both elements are important and should be given equal importance.

The Quran gives us guidance on how to achieve this balance. It encourages us to strive for excellence in all aspects of life and be mindful of our responsibilities both in the spiritual and mundane realms. It reminds us to be mindful of our actions and take responsibility for our actions and their consequences. Allah tells us in the Quran:

"And whatever good you do, (be sure) Allah knows it. And take a provision (with you) for the journey, but the best of provisions is fear of Allah. So fear Me, o men of understanding" (Surah Al-Baqarah: 2:197).

The Quran also instructs us to be mindful of our spiritual well-being and prioritize our relationship with Allah. It encourages us to seek guidance from Allah and remember Him in all our actions. Allah says in the Quran:

"Those who have faith and do righteous deeds, they are the best of creatures. Their reward is with Allah: Gardens of Eternity, beneath which rivers flow; they will dwell therein forever; Allah well-pleased with them, and they with Him: all this for such as fear their Lord and Cherisher" (Surah Al-Bayyinah: 98:7).

The Quran also reminds us to be mindful of our actions and take responsibility for our actions and their consequences. Allah says in the Quran:

"Say: 'Truly, my Lord enlarges and restricts the Sustenance to such of His servants as He pleases; and whatsoever you spend of anything (in Allah's Cause), He will replace it. And He is the Best of Providers'" (Surah Saba: 34:39).

Finally, the Quran encourages us to seek goodness in both this world and the next. Allah says:

Our Lord! Give us in this world that which is good and in the Hereafter that which is good, and save us from the torment of the Fire! (Surah Al-Baqarah- 2:201)

In conclusion, living a life of balance between the spiritual and the mundane is essential for leading a fulfilling life. It is possible to achieve this balance by following the teachings of the Qur'an and seeking guidance from Allah. The Quran encourages us to strive for excellence in all aspects of life and be mindful of our responsibilities both in the spiritual and mundane realms. It also reminds us to be mindful of our spiritual well-being and prioritize our relationship with Allah. Finally, it encourages us to seek goodness in both this world and the next. We can all strive to achieve this balance and lead a life of purpose and fulfillment.

16. Handling difficult situations in life with the help of the Qur'an

The Qur'an is an invaluable source of guidance for our modern lives. It offers a comprehensive outlook on life and provides spiritual, ethical, and healthful teachings that are applicable to all people, regardless of their religion or culture. In this chapter, we will explore how the Qur'an can help us to handle difficult situations in our lives, with a focus on the relevance of its teachings for modern day problems and stresses.

The Qur'an is a test and the book itself is a source of guidance for all of mankind, and it provides us with a clear path for handling difficult situations in life. The Qur'an provides us with a unique approach to dealing with adversity, and it reminds us to stay focused on our faith and keep our trust in Allah. In times of difficulty, the Qur'an encourages us to remain patient and steadfast, to seek the help of Allah, and to never lose hope.

The Qur'an reminds us that all things happen with the will of Allah, and that He is the one who ultimately controls our fate. We must remember that He is the source of all good and bad, and that He has a plan for us. The Qur'an teaches us that we must always remain patient and faithful, no matter what situation we may be in. We must remember that Allah never puts us in a situation that we cannot handle, and that He will provide us with strength and guidance if we turn to Him.

The Qur'an also encourages us to use the time of difficulty to grow spiritually, and to become closer to Allah. We must remember that our hardships have a purpose, and it is through them that we can learn and grow. We must also remember that Allah will always reward us for our patience and perseverance. The Qur'an teaches us that the ultimate reward for our faith and trust in Allah is paradise, and that we should strive to make it our ultimate goal.

The Qur'an also reminds us to remain humble and to seek help from Allah and from others in times of hardship. We must remember that no matter how difficult the situation may be, Allah is always there to help and guide us. We must also remember that there is no shame in seeking help from others, and that Allah will reward us for our humility and our willingness to seek assistance.

The Qur'an clearly outlines the proper ways to face and deal with difficulties, stressing that faith in Allah and patience are key elements. Here are 8 examples of how the Qur'an teaches us to deal with difficult situations:

1. Trust in Allah: "And whoever relies upon Allah - then He is sufficient for him" (Qur'an, 65:3). This verse teaches us that relying on Allah and trusting in Him is the best way to get through difficult times. We should not despair or feel overwhelmed because Allah is always there to support and help us.

2. Be Patient: *"O you who have believed, seek help through patience and prayer. Indeed, Allah is with the patient" (Qur'an, 2:153).* This verse stresses that patience is the key to overcoming difficult times. We should not

How to Live by The Qur'an

rush or give up in the face of adversity, but instead take the time to think and plan our actions.

3. Seek Help: If you seek help, seek it from Allah through repentance and be patient. Quran says *"And ask forgiveness of your Lord and then repent to Him. Indeed, my Lord is Merciful and Affectionate."* (Qur'an, 11:90). This verse encourages us to seek help from Allah and others in order to get through difficult times. We should not be ashamed to ask for help when we need it.

4. Turn to Allah: "And your Lord says, *'Call upon Me; I will respond to you'" (Qur'an, 40:60).* This verse reminds us to turn to Allah in times of difficulty, as He is always there to answer our prayers and provide comfort.

5. Have Faith: *"So be patient. Indeed, the promise of Allah is truth. And ask forgiveness for your sin and exalt [Allah] with praise of your Lord in the evening and the morning" (Qur'an, 40:55).* This verse teaches us to have faith in Allah and to persevere in difficult times. We should also seek His forgiveness and praise Him often.

6. Follow Guidance: *"Indeed, those who have believed and done righteous deeds – those are the best of creatures" (Qur'an, 98:7).* This verse reminds us to follow the guidance of Allah in order to get through difficult times. We should strive to be righteous and live according to the teachings of the Qur'an.

7. Make Du'a: *"And when My servants ask you, concerning Me – indeed I am near. I respond to the invocation of the supplicant when he calls upon Me" (Qur'an, 2:186).* This verse teaches us to make Du'a (supplication) to Allah in times of difficulty. We should

also remember that Allah is always near and will answer our prayers.

8. Rely on Allah: "And whoever relies upon Allah - then He is sufficient for him" (Qur'an, 65:3). This verse stresses that the best way to get through difficult times is to rely on Allah. He will provide us with everything we need and guide us through the darkness.

Overall, the Qur'an provides us with a clear path for dealing with difficult situations in life. It reminds us to remain patient and steadfast, to never lose hope, to use our time of difficulty to grow spiritually, and to seek help from Allah and from others. By following these guidelines, we can be sure that we are following the will of Allah, and that we will be rewarded

17. Keeping You and Your Family Healthy

Living a healthy life is a vital part of the Islamic faith. The Qur'an provides guidance to believers on how to maintain their physical, mental and spiritual health. By following the teachings of the Qur'an, believers can ensure that they and their families remain healthy and strong.

The Qur'an provides clear instructions on how we should look after our physical health. It is important to realize that health is a gift from Allah and should be preserved and respected. The Qur'an encourages us to *"eat of the good things which We have provided for you" (2:172).*

The Qur'an recommends that believers consume a variety of foods, including fruits and vegetables, grains, dairy products, and halal meats. Fruits and vegetables are particularly important for health, as they contain essential vitamins and minerals that are essential for good health. The Qur'an states, *"And of the fruits of the palms and grapes, you obtain wholesome drink and nourishment. Indeed in that is a sign for a people who reason" (16:67).* The Qur'an also instructs believers to eat in moderation, so as not to overindulge. The Qur'an states, *"Eat of the good things We have provided for you, but commit no excess therein" (20:81).*

The Qur'an also emphasizes the importance of personal hygiene. The Qur'an states, *"Verily, Allah loves those who turn to Him in repentance and loves those who purify themselves" (2:222).* The Qur'an urges us to keep our bodies and clothes clean and to practice good hygiene habits. Qur'an helps us identify what foods are beneficial for us; honey (16: 68-69), vegetables such as corn and herbs (55:12, 80:27-32) and fruits such as olives, dates, grapes, pomegranates (6: 99,141), and bananas (56: 29).

Quran also recommended us to eat the meat of certain animals and their milk, as well as fresh fish and birds; *"He created cattle for you, wherein is warmth and many gains, and you eat thereof" (16:5, 22:28);*

"For you there is in the cattle a lesson; We give you to drink what is in their bellies from betwixt the chime and the blood pure milk, easy and palatable for those who drink it" (16:66).

"He it is Who made the sea of service that you might eat fresh (fish) meat from it" (16:14, 35:12).

"And the meat of fowls of what they like" (56:21)

In addition to physical health, the Qur'an also addresses mental and spiritual health. The Qur'an encourages believers to have faith in Allah and to seek comfort and solace in the remembrance of Him. The Qur'an states, *"O you who believe! When you rise up for prayer, wash your faces, and your hands up to the elbows, and wipe your heads, and your feet to the ankles" (5:6).* This is a reminder to believers that prayer and worship are essential for good mental and spiritual health.

The Qur'an also emphasizes the importance of avoiding wasteful behaviour. The Qur'an states, *"Do not waste: verily, Allah does not love the wasteful" (7:31).* Wasteful behaviour includes consuming more than

How to Live by The Qur'an

necessary, wasting food, and wasting resources. It is important to remember that being wasteful is a sin in Islam, and that believers should strive to conserve resources and not be wasteful.

Finally, the Qur'an emphasizes the importance of looking after one another. The Qur'an states, *"And help one another in righteousness and piety" (5:2)*. This is a reminder to believers that they should look after the health and well-being of their families and communities. This includes providing for their families, taking care of their health, and looking out for one another. Allah also says, *Do not with your own hands throw yourself into ruin" (2:195),* meaning that we should not consume anything that can bring destruction for us, both physically and spiritually.

In conclusion, the Qur'an provides guidance to believers on how to maintain their physical, mental, and spiritual health. It encourages believers to eat a healthy and balanced diet, practice good hygiene habits, and take care of one another. By following the teachings of the Qur'an, believers can ensure that they and their families remain healthy and strong.

18. The Qur'an and Ecology: A Call for Stewardship of the Earth

The Qur'an establishes a clear link between humans and the environment, declaring that everything in the universe is part of a harmonious and interconnected order. Thus, the Qur'an outlines a holistic view of ecology, emphasizing the need to protect the environment, and calling on believers to take responsibility for the stewardship of the earth.

The Qur'an recognizes the Creator as the ultimate source of all life and the environment, and as such, it contains numerous teachings that promote respect for the environment. In one passage, Allah says: *"He it is Who appointed the sun a splendor and the moon a light, and measured for her stages, that you might know the number of years and the reckoning" (Qur'an 10:5)*. Allah is presented as the one who has created and provided for the environment and engaged the human beings as His vicegerent on earth. Therefore, humans should be the one that is held accountable for its upkeep.

The Qur'an also contains many verses that discuss the need to take care of the environment and to protect it from harm. Allah says: *"And the earth, He has assigned it for all living creatures" (Qur'an 55:10)*. This verse highlights the importance of conserving the natural resources of the earth and using them responsibly. Furthermore, Allah says: *"And do not abuse the earth, spreading corruption" (Qur'an 2:60)*. This verse emphasizes the need to protect the environment from human-caused pollution and destruction.

In addition to the need to protect the environment, the Qur'an calls on believers to take responsibility for the stewardship of the earth. In the Qur'an, Allah says: *"And He has made of service to you whatsoever is in the heavens and whatsoever is in the earth; it is all from Him" (Qur'an 45:13)*. This verse encourages believers to recognize their responsibility to care for the environment and to use its resources wisely.

The Qur'an also outlines the importance of protecting animals, plants, and other living things. In one passage, Allah says: *"There is not an animal (that lives) on the earth, nor a being that flies on its wings, but (forms part of) communities like you" (Qur'an 6:38)*. This passage underscores the importance of protecting all forms of life and emphasizes the need to respect each other's rights. Similarly, in another passage, Allah says: *"And there is not a thing but its (sources and) treasures (inexhaustible) are with Us. But We only send down thereof in due and ascertainable measures" (Qur'an 15:21)*. This verse highlights the need to conserve natural resources and to use them responsibly.

The Qur'an also outlines the importance of maintaining a balance between humans and the environment. Allah says: *"And it is He Who sends down rain from the sky, and with it We bring forth vegetation of all kinds; out of it We bring forth green (crops) out of which We produce grain, heaped up (in barns)" (Qur'an 6:99)*. This verse emphasizes the need to maintain a balance between human activity and the environment, recognizing that humans are dependent on the environment for their sustenance.

The Qur'an encourages believers to develop an understanding of the environment and to appreciate its beauty. In one passage, Allah says: *"Do you not see that Allah makes the night to enter into the day and He makes the day to enter into the night" (Qur'an 31:29).* This verse emphasizes the importance of appreciating the beauty of the environment and encourages believers to recognize the delicate balance between humans and the environment.

The Qur'an also outlines the need to take responsibility for the stewardship of the earth. In one passage, Allah says: *"We have honoured the sons of Adam; provided them with transport on land and sea; given them for sustenance things good and pure; and conferred on them special favours, above a great part of our Creation" (Qur'an 17:70).* This verse illustrates the importance of taking responsibility for the care and protection of the environment as the most favoured species of the Almighty creator.

The Qur'an emphasizes the need to work together to protect the environment and to ensure sustainability. Allah says: *"And cooperate in righteousness and piety, but do not cooperate in sin and aggression" (Qur'an 5:2).* This verse calls on believers to work together to protect the environment and to ensure its future sustainability.

In conclusion, the Qur'an outlines a holistic view of ecology, emphasizing the need to protect the environment and calling on believers to take responsibility for the stewardship of the earth. The

How to Live by The Qur'an

Qur'an recognizes the Creator as the ultimate source of all life and the environment, and as such, it contains numerous teachings that promote respect for the environment and emphasize the need to take care of the environment and to protect it from harm. Furthermore, the Qur'an calls on believers to take responsibility for the stewardship of the earth, to protect animals, plants, and other living things, to maintain a balance between humans and the environment, and to work together to protect the environment and to ensure sustainability. The Qur'an's teachings on ecology provide a powerful reminder of the importance of preserving our environment and of taking responsibility for its stewardship.

19. Dealing with Stress and Anxiety: The Qur'an's Perspective

Stress and anxiety are inevitable aspects of life in the modern world and can take a toll on our physical and mental health. While some amount of stress is necessary to fulfill our goals, too much can be debilitating and can have a negative impact on our wellbeing. That's why it is important to develop effective strategies for managing stress and anxiety. In this chapter, we will explore the Qur'an's perspective on dealing with stress and anxiety.

The Qur'an is a source of spiritual guidance and wisdom that can help us cope with stress and anxiety in the modern world. Throughout the Qur'an, Allah reminds us to be patient and seek His help during times of difficulty. He (SWT) also encourages us to reflect on the blessings that we have been given and to count our blessings. As the Qur'an states, *"...And remember your Lord within yourself, humbly and with fear and without loudness in words, in the mornings and in the evenings; and be not of those who are neglectful."* (7:205)

The Qur'an also teaches us to trust in Allah and to take refuge in Him during times of distress. As the Qur'an states, *"...And when they (the believers) have to pass through distress, they say: 'Truly, to Allah we belong and truly, to Him shall we return.'"* (2:156) By trusting in Allah and seeking refuge in Him, we can find strength and courage to face our anxieties and stress.

In addition, the Qur'an encourages us to turn to Allah in prayer and supplication. As the Qur'an states,

"And your Lord said: 'Invoke Me, I will respond to your invocation." (40:60). By turning to Allah in prayer and supplication, we can seek His guidance and help during times of distress.

The Qur'an also emphasizes the importance of having a positive attitude and outlook on life. As the Qur'an states, *"...Verily, Allah does not change the condition of a people until they change what is in themselves." (13:11)* By changing our outlook and attitude, we can make an effort to find peace and joy in the midst of our stress and anxiety.

The Qur'an also teaches us to be thankful and grateful for the blessings that we have been given. As the Qur'an states, *"...And be thankful to Allah, if it is Him that you worship." (2:172)* By being thankful and grateful, we can find peace and joy in the midst of our stress and anxiety.

The Qur'an also teaches us to remain focused on the Hereafter and to keep our faith strong in the face of trials and tribulations. As the Qur'an states, *"...And remember the favour of Allah upon you, and His covenant which He made with you, when you said: 'We hear and we obey.' And fear Allah; surely, Allah is aware of the innermost secrets of your hearts." (5:7)* By keeping our faith strong, we can find peace and strength in the midst of our stress and anxiety.

The Qur'an also encourages us to be patient and to persevere in the face of adversity. As the Qur'an states, "...And be patient and persevering, for Allah is with those who patiently persevere." (2:153) By remaining patient and persevering, we can find strength and courage to face our anxieties and stress.

Finally, the Qur'an teaches us to seek help from Allah in times of need. As the Qur'an states, *"...And when We want to destroy a town, We (first) command its people who lead easy lives, but they transgress therein; thus the word (of torment) is justified against it, and We destroy it with utter destruction."* (17:16) By seeking help from Allah, and understanding His commands given through this Quran, we can find strength and courage to face our anxieties and stress.

In conclusion, the Qur'an offers practical guidance and wisdom on dealing with stress and anxiety in the modern world. It encourages us to be patient and seek Allah's (SWT) help during times of difficulty. It also teaches us to trust in Allah, to turn to Him in prayer and supplication, to have a positive attitude and outlook on life, to be thankful and grateful for the blessings that we have been given, to remain focused on the Hereafter, and to seek help from Allah in times of need. By following the teachings of the Qur'an, we can find strength and courage to face our anxieties and stress.

20. The Qur'an and Self-Improvement: Developing Mental and Spiritual Strength

The Qur'an is an invaluable source of guidance and inspiration for believers in their pursuit of self-improvement. The Qur'an speaks of the importance of developing mental and spiritual strength in order to live a life of faith and righteousness. The Qur'an contains numerous verses that highlight the importance of self-improvement and offer guidance to believers on how to achieve it.

The Qur'an states that the believers should "guard themselves against evil" because *' o believers, you are only accountable for yourselves (Qur'an 5:105)*. This verse emphasizes the importance of self-improvement as it calls upon believers to continuously strive to improve themselves. The Qur'an further states that believers should take time to reflect on their own conduct and strive to make improvements based on their reflections (*ref: Allah commands you to return trusts to their rightful owners; and when you judge between people, judge with fairness. What a noble commandment from Allah to you! Qur'an 4:58)*. This verse encourages the believers to use their time and resources wisely in order to practice fairness and justice thereby improving themselves and attaining spiritual growth.

The Qur'an also urges the believers to be patient and persevering in their pursuit of self-improvement. The Qur'an states that believers should *"be patient, for indeed Allah does not waste the reward of those who do* good" (Qur'an 11:115). This verse highlights the importance of being patient and steadfast in the pursuit of self-improvement or whatever situation a believer faces. The Qur'an also states that believers should be mindful of their thoughts and actions, as these will determine their ultimate success or failure *(O believers! Be mindful of Allah and let every soul look to what ˹deeds˺ it has sent forth for tomorrow. And fear Allah, ˹for˺ certainly Allah is All-Aware of what you do. (Qur'an 59:18)*. This verse emphasizes the importance of being mindful of one's thoughts and actions, as these can have a profound impact on one's life.

The Qur'an also encourages believers to develop a sense of humility and moderation in their pursuit of self-improvement. The Qur'an states that believers should "not be too proud of themselves" as Quran says *...so (as for) those who do not believe in the hereafter, their hearts are ignorant, and they are proud" (Quran 16:22)*.

By equating the concepts of ignorance with having pride, the Quran teaches us that to have pride itself is to be blatantly ignorant. We must not become those who from meaningless pride and arrogance become embarrassingly ignorant and forget our true purpose in life: to worship Allah alone in everything that we do here on earth. This verse highlights the importance of humility and moderation in the pursuit of self-improvement. The Qur'an further states that believers should *"strive for the best in deeds" (Qur'an 28:77)*. This verse encourages believers to strive for excellence in their pursuit of self-improvement.

The Qur'an also encourages believers to seek knowledge and wisdom in their pursuit of self-improvement. The Qur'an states that believers should pray "increase me in knowledge" (Qur'an 20:114). This verse emphasizes the importance of seeking knowledge and wisdom in the pursuit of self-improvement. The Qur'an further states that believers should "ask those who possess knowledge if you do not know" (Qur'an 16:43). This verse encourages believers to seek knowledge from the professionals in their pursuit of self-improvement.

The Qur'an also encourages believers to practice self-discipline in their pursuit of self-improvement. The Qur'an states that believers should *"guard their own souls" (Qur'an 5:105).* This verse emphasizes the importance of self-discipline in the pursuit of self-improvement. The Qur'an further states that believers should *"take what the Messenger assigns to you, and refrain from that which he withholds from you. And fear Allah; for Allah is strict in Punishment." (Qur'an 59:7).* This verse encourages believers to practice self-discipline and refrain from engaging in activities that are forbidden by Allah and His messenger.

The Qur'an also encourages believers to foster a positive attitude in their pursuit of self-improvement. The Qur'an states that believers should "look upon the good things with gratitude" because *"If you tried to count Allah's blessings, you would never be able to number them. Surely Allah is All-Forgiving, Most Merciful (Qur'an 16:18).* This verse highlights the importance of maintaining a positive, grateful attitude in the pursuit of self-improvement. The Qur'an further states that believers should *"seek help through patience and prayer" (Qur'an 2:45).* This verse encourages believers to remain patient and seek help from Allah in their pursuit of self-improvement.

The Qur'an also encourages believers to be mindful of their speech and strive to speak only that which is beneficial. The Qur'an states that believers should *"always speak with words that which is best" (Qur'an 17:53).* This verse emphasizes the importance of speaking with kindness and justice in the pursuit of self-improvement. The Qur'an further states that believers should *"speak with fairness" (Qur'an 33:70).* This verse encourages believers to speak with fairness and justice in their pursuit of self-improvement.

The Qur'an also encourages believers to foster a sense of thankfulness in their pursuit of self-improvement. The Qur'an states that believers should "give thanks to Allah for all of His blessings" *("If you give thanks, I will certainly grant you more; but if you are ungrateful for My favours, My chastisement is terrible. (Qur'an 14:7).* This verse emphasizes the importance of being thankful for all of the blessings that Allah has bestowed upon us.

The Qur'an also encourages believers to seek help from Allah in their pursuit of self-improvement. The Qur'an states that believers should always "seek help from Allah" because *'If Allah touches you with harm, none can undo it except Him. And if He intends good for you, none can withhold His bounty. He grants it to whoever He wills of His servants. And He is the All-*

Forgiving, Most Merciful. (Qur'an 10:107). This verse emphasizes the importance of seeking help from Allah in the pursuit of self-improvement. The Qur'an further states that believers should "ask for Allah's help in all things" (Qur'an 2:186). This verse encourages believers to seek help from Allah in all things, as He is the source of all good.

The Qur'an is an invaluable source of guidance and inspiration for believers in their pursuit of self-improvement. The Qur'an speaks of the importance of developing mental and spiritual strength in order to live a life of faith and righteousness. The Qur'an contains numerous verses that highlight the importance of self-improvement and offer guidance to believers on how to achieve it. By reflecting on the guidance contained in the Qur'an, believers can make strides towards achieving the highest level of personal development and spiritual growth.

21. Developing a Positive Attitude: Overcoming Negative Thinking

The Qur'an is a book of guidance, and it is our duty to live by it. We must strive to develop a positive attitude and overcome any negative thinking in order to truly live by the Qur'an in the modern times. There are several ways to do this, and in this chapter we will discuss some of the most important ones.

First and foremost, we must strive to be patient and have faith in Allah. The Qur'an says: *"O you who have believed, seek help through patience and prayer. Indeed, Allah is with the patient." (Qur'an 2:153)* Patience is a virtue and it's essential for overcoming negative thoughts and feelings. We must have faith that Allah knows what is best for us and will provide us with the strength to get through any tribulations we face.

Second, we must strive to maintain a positive outlook and attitude at all times. The Qur'an says: *"...and indeed, Allah loves those who are constantly conscious of Him" (Qur'an 3:76).* We must remember to always give thanks to Allah and be grateful for all that He has provided us. This will help us maintain a positive attitude in our lives.

Third, we must make an effort to always think positive and be optimistic. The Qur'an says: *"Verily, with hardship, comes ease." (Qur'an 94:5-6)* We must remember that every difficulty that we face will eventually pass, and that Allah will provide us with the strength to

How to Live by The Qur'an

get through it. With this in mind, we should strive to stay positive and optimistic.

Fourth, we must strive to avoid negative thinking and focus on the good. The Qur'an says: *"Verily, Allah does not change the condition of a people until they change what is in themselves." (Qur'an 13:11)* We must strive to focus on the good in our lives and find ways to make the most out of our situations. This will help us stay positive and be content with our lives.

Fifth, we must strive to be kind and compassionate to ourselves and to others. The Qur'an says: *"...and spend of your substance in the cause of Allah, and make not your own hands contribute to your destruction; but do good; for Allah loves those who do good." (Qur'an 2:195)* We must strive to be kind to ourselves and others, and to do good deeds. This will help us stay positive and be content with our lives.

Finally, we must strive to remember that Allah is the Most Merciful and that He will always be there for us. The Qur'an says: *"...and seek help through patience and prayer, and indeed, it is difficult except for the humbly submissive [to Allah]" (Qur'an 2:45).* We must remember that Allah is always with us and He will provide us with the strength to get through any tribulations we face.

In conclusion, we must strive to develop a positive attitude and overcome any negative thinking in order to truly live by the Qur'an in the modern times. We must remember to be patient and have faith in Allah, to maintain a positive outlook and attitude, to think positively and be optimistic, to avoid negative thinking and focus on the good, to be kind and compassionate to ourselves and to others, and to remember that Allah is the Most Merciful and He will always be there for us. By following these steps, we can strive to truly live by the Qur'an in the modern times.

22. Tolerance and Respect: Interacting with People of Different Faiths

Living in a modern, globalized world, Muslims are constantly interacting with people of other faiths, cultures, and backgrounds. In such a diverse and interconnected environment, it is important for Muslims to demonstrate tolerance and respect towards people of other beliefs and backgrounds. The Quran encourages Muslims to be respectful to those of other faiths, and to strive for peaceful coexistence with them.

The Quran states that *"there is no compulsion in religion" (2:256)* and that *"to each of you We prescribed a law and a way" (5:48)*. These verses remind us that no one has the authority to force someone to accept a particular faith and that each person has the right to practice their own faith. This principle of freedom of belief and respect for different faiths is enshrined in the Quran and should be upheld by Muslims in their daily lives.

The Quran also states that *"They are not all alike. Of the People of the Scripture there is a staunch community who recite the revelations of Allah in the night season, falling prostrate (before Him)." (3:113)*. This verse reminds us that there may still be some people who clandestinely submits themselves to Allah and that believers of different faiths can coexist peacefully and collaborate in good works. Muslims should strive to create bridges of understanding and mutual respect with people of other faiths, and work together to promote justice and peace in the world.

The Quran also states that *"O mankind, indeed We have created you from male and female and made you peoples and tribes that you may know one another. Indeed, the most noble of you in the sight of Allāh is the most righteous1 of you. Indeed, Allāh is Knowing and Aware." (49:13)*. This verse reminds us that all people are equal in the eyes of Allah and should be treated with respect and kindness, regardless of their faith or background.

The Quran also states that *"Cooperate with one another in goodness and righteousness, and do not cooperate in sin and transgression. And be mindful of Allah. Surely Allah is severe in punishment." (Quran 5:2)*. This verse encourages Muslims to collaborate with people of other faiths in promoting justice and goodness, and to refrain from participating in any activities that could lead to hatred and division.

The Quran also states that *"Allah does not forbid you from those who do not fight you because of religion and do not expel you from your homes – from being righteous toward them and acting justly toward them. Indeed, Allah loves those who act justly" (Quran 60:8)*. This verse reminds us that Muslims should treat people of other faiths with justice and kindness, and that even in times of conflict, Muslims should strive for peace and understanding.

The Quran also states that *"If they are inclined towards peace, make peace with them. And put your trust in Allah. Indeed, He ˹alone˺ is the All-Hearing, All-*

Knowing."(Quran 8:61). This verse encourages Muslims to strive for peace and understanding with people of other faiths, and to trust in Allah's ultimate wisdom and judgment.

The Quran also states that *"Allah loves those who are patient" (3:146)* and that *"if any do deeds of righteousness – be they male or female – and have faith, they will enter heaven, and not the least injustice will be done to them" (4:124).* These verses remind us that Allah rewards those who are patient and tolerant, and that justice and fairness are essential in our interactions with people of other faiths.

The Quran also states that *"and dispute ye not with the People of the Book, except in the best manner" (29:46).* This verse encourages Muslims to engage in respectful dialogue and debate with people of other faiths, and to strive for understanding and mutual respect.

Finally, the Quran reminds us that *"Allah does not forbid you from showing kindness and dealing justly with those who have not fought you because of religion and have not driven you out of your homes" (60:8).* This verse encourages Muslims to be kind and just to people of other faiths, and to strive for peaceful coexistence with them.

In conclusion, the Quran encourages Muslims to demonstrate tolerance and respect towards people of other beliefs and backgrounds. Muslims should strive to create bridges of understanding and mutual respect with people of other faiths, and work together to promote justice and peace in the world. Muslims should also strive for patience and understanding when engaging with people of other faiths, and trust in Allah's ultimate wisdom and judgment. By demonstrating tolerance and respect towards people of other faiths, Muslims can foster a world of peace, justice, and understanding.

23. The Qur'an and Social Justice: Building a Better Society

Social justice is a concept that has been around for centuries, but it has taken on greater importance in the 21st century. With the rapid growth of globalization, economic inequality, and racism, social justice has become an increasingly important topic in today's society. The Qur'an, being the main source of Islamic law, is a great source to turn to in order to understand how to build a better society and achieve social justice. The Qur'an contains numerous verses that speak to the importance of justice, fairness, and equity. This chapter will explore how the Qur'an's teachings can be applied to modern society in order to achieve social justice in the 21st century.

Justice in the Qur'an

The concept of justice is a recurring theme in the Qur'an. In Surah al-Ma'idah, Allah says, *"O you who have believed, be persistently standing firm in justice, witnesses for Allah, even if it be against yourselves or parents and relatives. Whether one is rich or poor, Allah is more worthy of both. So follow not [personal] inclination, lest you not be just. And if you distort [your testimony] or refuse [to give it], then indeed Allah is ever, with what you do, Acquainted" (Qur'an 5:8)*. This verse emphasizes the importance of justice for all and the need to be impartial regardless of one's own interests or biases. It also highlights the importance of truthfulness and honesty in testimony and the need to follow Allah's commands even if it goes against one's own desires.

Furthermore, in Surah al-An'am, Allah says, *"And do not come near the wealth of the orphan—unless intending to enhance it—until they attain maturity. Give full measure and weigh with justice. We never require of any soul more than what it can afford. Whenever you speak, maintain justice—even regarding a close relative. And fulfil your covenant with Allah. This is what He has commanded you, so perhaps you will be mindful." (Qur'an 6:152).* This verse further emphasizes the importance of justice and fairness. It also speaks to the need to be honest and truthful in all dealings with the property of orphans and to not be swayed by personal desires.

These verses from the Qur'an demonstrate the importance of justice and fairness and are a clear call for Muslims to strive for social justice in the modern world.

Justice and Equality

The Qur'an emphasizes the importance of justice and fairness in all dealings and forbids the oppression of any group of people. In Surah al-Hujurat, Allah says, *"O mankind, indeed We have created you from male and female and made you peoples and tribes that you may know one another. Indeed, the most noble of you in the sight of Allah is the most righteous of you. Indeed, Allah is Knowing and Acquainted" (Qur'an 49:13).* This verse emphasizes the importance of treating all people with respect and dignity regardless of their race, gender, religion, or social class.

How to Live by The Qur'an

These verses from the Qur'an demonstrate the need for equality and justice for all people and are a clear call for Muslims to strive for social justice in the modern world.

Compassion and Mercy

The Qur'an also emphasizes the importance of compassion and mercy in all dealings. In Surah al-Baqarah, Allah says, *"And We have certainly made the Qur'an easy for remembrance, so is there any who will remember?" (Qur'an 54:17).* This verse emphasizes the importance of following the Quran verses as a reference point in dealing with others and highlights the need to be understanding and forgiving.

The Qur'an is a great source of guidance for Muslims in the 21st century. It contains numerous verses that speak to the importance of justice, fairness, and equity. It also emphasizes the need to treat all people with respect and dignity, to be compassionate and merciful, and to strive for social justice. The teachings of the Qur'an can be applied to modern society in order to make it a better place and to achieve social justice in the 21st century.

24. The Qur'an and Politics: A Framework for a Just Society

The Qur'an provides an invaluable guide for how to lead a just and moral life in the modern world. In addition to these spiritual and moral teachings, the Qur'an also provides a framework for how to engage in politics and establish a just society. However, Quran is not a book of politics except its appeal for a value-based society based on some universal principles which may have some political implications in our times. Quran does also make mention of few concepts such as "the oppressed" (mustad'afeen), "emigration" (hijra), the "Muslim community" (Ummah), and "fighting" or "struggling" in the way of God (jihād) which have some connotations with modern nations states.

Nevertheless, Qur'an outlines a number of principles that should be followed in political life. The most fundamental of these is the belief in the oneness of Allah, and accepting Him as the supreme law giver as expressed in verse 3:18: *"Allah Himself bears witness that there is no God but He; and likewise do the angels and the men possessed of knowledge bear witness in truth and justice that there is no God but He, the All-Mighty, the All-Wise"(Quran 3:18).* This belief is the foundation of all Islamic teachings and informs the principles of justice, equality, and compassion that are promoted in the Qur'an.

The Qur'an also emphasizes the importance of justice in political life. Verse 4:58 states: *"Indeed, Allah commands you to render trusts to whom they are due and when you judge between people to judge with justice. Excellent is that which Allah instructs you. Indeed, Allah is ever Hearing and Seeing."*. This verse highlights the importance of fairness and impartiality in political decision-making and the need to treat all people equally.

Furthermore, the Qur'an promotes the concept of consultation as a means of establishing a just society. A chapter in the Quran is named Shura and in it God emphasizes the desired attributes of the faithful, including *"those who answer the call of their Lord and establish worship, and whose affairs are a matter of counsel, and who spend of what We have bestowed on them"*. (42:38)

Consulting others, or Mashwara, was a practice of the Holy Prophet (s). He taught the Muslims to follow it in their own daily lives. Through this practice, the Prophet (s) nurtured higher level thinking among the Muslims, teaching them that they could also contribute to the running of the affairs in the Muslim society

Verse 3:159 states: *"Therefore, by your Lord, We will surely question them all, as to what they have been doing"*. This verse highlights the responsibility of the political leaders, but good leaders can exonerate themselves by consulting with those affected by decisions and ensuring their input is taken into account, according to aforementioned verse 42:38.

In addition to promoting justice and consultation, the Qur'an also encourages the development of a sense of compassion and mercy in political life. Verse 2:83 states: *"And when We grant mercy from Us to any people, they rejoice in it; and there is no help for those who neglect Our mercy"*. This verse teaches us that a just society should be guided by compassion and mercy, rather than by fear or coercion.

The Qur'an also outlines a number of principles that should be followed in order to ensure the safety and security of the people. Verse 8:60 states: *"And make ready against them whatever you can of power and of steeds of war, to terrify the enemy of Allah and your enemy, and others besides them whom you do not know"*. This verse highlights the importance of having the necessary resources and capabilities to protect the people and maintain peace and security.

Finally, the Qur'an promotes the concept of accountability and responsibility in political life. Verse 4:58 states: *"Verily, Allah holds those in authority responsible for their actions"*. This verse emphasises the need for those in positions of power to take responsibility for their decisions and be held accountable for their actions.

In conclusion, the Qur'an provides a framework for establishing a just society in the modern world. This framework is based on principles of justice, consultation, compassion, security, and accountability. When these principles are followed, they can create an environment of justice, fairness, and equality, which will benefit all people.

25. Living with Patience and Resilience: How to Overcome Difficulties

Living with patience and resilience is essential in order to overcome difficulties in life. The Qur'an is a source of divine wisdom and guidance that can help us to develop these qualities. It teaches us to be patient and resilient in difficult times and provides us with the tools we need to cope with life's challenges.

Patience is a virtue that is highly praised in the Qur'an. Allah says in Surah Al-Baqarah, *"O believers! Seek comfort in patience and prayer. Allah is truly with those who are patient." (2:153)*. Patience is an important part of faith and is a necessary requirement for those who want to live by the Qur'an. By possessing patience, we will be able to bear the hardships and trials of life in a positive and constructive way.

The Qur'an also encourages us to be resilient in the face of adversity. Allah says in Surah Al-Anfal, *"Obey Allah and His Messenger and do not dispute with one another, or you would be discouraged and weakened. Persevere! Surely Allah is with those who persevere." (8:46)*. Persevere in this verse means *Be steadfast in the face of adversity and strive to excel in good deeds*. This verse shows us that we should never give up in the face of difficulties, but rather strive to do our best and stay positive by following the commands of Allah and examples of the prophet (pbuh).

In order to develop patience and resilience, it is important to remember that Allah is the ultimate source of strength and comfort. He (SWT) says in Surah Al-Hijr, *"And whoever puts their trust in Allah, then He ˹alone˺ is sufficient for them. Certainly Allah achieves His Will. Allah has already set a destiny for everything. (65:3)*. We should always keep this in mind and turn to Him (Allah) in prayer and supplication whenever we are faced with difficult times.

The Qur'an also encourages us to develop a sense of gratitude and contentment in order to cope with life's difficulties. Allah says in Surah Ar-Rum, *"If you are grateful, I will surely increase you [in favor]; but if you deny, indeed, My punishment is severe." (14:07)*. Gratitude helps us to appreciate the blessings we have and the good things in our lives, even in the midst of difficulties.

In addition to developing patience and resilience, the Qur'an also teaches us to remain hopeful in the face of adversity. Allah says in Surah Al-Inshirah, *"Surely with difficulty comes ease" (94:5)*. This verse reminds us that although we may encounter difficult times, we should never give up hope, as Allah promises that He will always help us through our difficulties.

The Qur'an also encourages us to use our time wisely by engaging in activities that bring us closer to Allah. Allah says in Surah At-Talaq, *"And whosoever fears Allah and keeps his duty to Him, He will make a way for him to get out (from every difficulty). And He will provide him from (sources) he never could imagine. (65:2-3)*. This verse reminds us that if we make Allah our priority and focus on obedience to Him, He will make our path easy and open up the doors of success for us.

How to Live by The Qur'an

The Qur'an also teaches us to practice self-discipline and control our emotions in order to cope with life's difficulties. Allah says in Surah Al-Baqara, *"O you who have faith, seek help with patient perseverance and prayer" (2:45)*. This verse reminds us that we should control our emotions and be patient in the face of difficulties.

The Qur'an encourages us to remain steadfast in our faith and to trust in Allah. Living with patience and resilience is essential in order to overcome difficulties in life. The Qur'an is a source of divine wisdom and guidance that can help us to develop these qualities. By possessing patience, resilience, gratitude and contentment, self-discipline, and trust in Allah, we can better cope with life's hardships and remain steadfast in our faith.

26. Finding Peace and Contentment: The Qur'an's Perspective

The Qur'an is a book that was revealed to Prophet Muhammad (peace be upon him) over 1400 years ago, yet it contains timeless advice that is just as relevant to modern society today as it was when it was first revealed. One of the most important themes in the Qur'an is the importance of finding peace and contentment in this life and the hereafter. The Qur'an provides guidance on how to achieve this important goal and offers a unique perspective on how to live a life of tranquility and contentment.

The Qur'an teaches us that true peace and contentment come from Allah and that it is only through Him that we can achieve these goals. Allah says in the Qur'an: *"And those who have faith and do righteous deeds, they are the best of creatures. Their reward with Allah is gardens of eternity, beneath which rivers flow, wherein they shall abide forever; a gift from Allah. And that which is with Allah is best for the righteous" (Qur'an 98:7-8).* This verse of the Qur'an is a reminder that true peace and contentment come only from Allah.

The Qur'an also emphasizes the importance of maintaining a positive attitude and outlook in life. Allah says in the Qur'an: *"And seek help through patience and prayer, and indeed it is difficult except for the humbly submissive [to Allah]" (Qur'an 2:45).* This verse is a reminder that patience and prayer are key elements of achieving peace and contentment.

How to Live by The Qur'an

The Qur'an also emphasizes the importance of engaging in righteous deeds and avoiding sin. Allah says in the Qur'an: *"And [by] the soul and He who proportioned it and inspired it [with discernment of] its wickedness and its righteousness, he has succeeded who purifies it, and he has failed who instills it [with corruption]" (Qur'an 91:7-10).* This verse of the Qur'an is a reminder that engaging in righteous deeds and avoiding sin are essential components of achieving true peace and contentment in life.

The Qur'an also emphasizes the importance of having a proper and balanced view of the world. Allah says in the Qur'an: *"And it is thus that We appointed you to be the community of the middle way so that you might be witnesses to all mankind and the Messenger might be a witness to you". (Qur'an 2:143).* This verse of the Qur'an is a reminder that we should strive to find balance in life and not let our emotions and desires lead us astray. The word wasatā means the middle point between two things. It is also used to refer to something beautiful and honorable. That is because anything that is balanced and not extreme in either direction is admirable.

Balance is required in all aspects of life. In beliefs, Islam emphasizes that God is not completely controlling of the actions of the human being, nor does He leave everything to the human being. Humans are given limited autonomy with a free will and it is their discretion to make a balance between their choices. Lifestyle must be balanced between material and spiritual. Believers should not be so immersed in worldly matters that they ignore the spiritual, nor should they focus on spirituality so much and abandon the world. Many verses of Quran talk about balance. Regarding salāt Allah says: Be neither loud in your prayer nor murmur it, but follow a middle course between these (Q 17:110). About spending He says: Those who when spending are neither wasteful nor tightfisted and keep between these two [extremes] (Q 25:67).

The Qur'an also emphasizes the importance of maintaining a healthy lifestyle and taking care of one's physical and mental health. Allah says in the Qur'an: *"And eat and drink but waste not by extravagance, certainly He does not love the extravagant" (Qur'an 7:31)*. This verse of the Qur'an is a reminder that we should strive to maintain a healthy lifestyle and take care of our physical and mental health.

The Qur'an also emphasizes the importance of having a sense of gratitude and thankfulness in life. Allah says in the Qur'an: *"And [remember] when your Lord proclaimed, 'If you are grateful, I will surely increase you [in favour]; but if you deny, indeed, My punishment is severe'" (Qur'an 14:7)*. This verse of the Qur'an is a reminder that we should strive to be thankful for the blessings that Allah has bestowed upon us.

The Qur'an also emphasizes the importance of having a strong faith in Allah. Allah says in the Qur'an: *"And whoever puts his trust in Allah, He will suffice him" (Qur'an 65:3)*. This verse of the Qur'an is a reminder that true peace and contentment come from having a strong faith in Allah.

How to Live by The Qur'an

The Qur'an also emphasizes the importance of being patient and persevering in the face of trials and tribulations. Allah says in the Qur'an: *"O you who have believed, be patient and seek help through patience and prayer. Indeed, Allah is with the patient" (Qur'an 2:153)*. This verse of the Qur'an is a reminder that true peace and contentment come from having patience and perseverance in the face of adversity.

The Qur'an also emphasizes the importance of having a good relationship with Allah. Allah says in the Qur'an: *"And He is with you wherever you are. And Allah is Seeing of what you do" (Qur'an 57:4)*. This verse of the Qur'an is a reminder that you are always under the watchful eyes of your creator Allah, and since you have submitted to Him sincerely and He is always with you wherever you go, you can expect to enjoy true peace and contentment by forming a strong relationship with Allah.

Finally, the Qur'an emphasizes the importance of living a life of moderation and avoiding extremes. Allah says in the Qur'an: *"O you who have believed, avoid much [negative] assumption. Indeed, some assumption is sin. And do not spy or backbite each other. Would one of you like to eat the flesh of his brother when dead? You would detest it. And fear Allah; indeed, Allah is Accepting of repentance and Merciful" (Qur'an 49:12)*. This verse of the Qur'an is a reminder that true peace and contentment come from avoiding extremes, (such as being judgmental, having suspicions about others, backbiting, ill speeches etc) and living a life of moderation and balance.

In conclusion, the Qur'an provides timeless advice on how to achieve true peace and contentment in life. The Qur'an emphasizes the importance of having faith in Allah, engaging in righteous deeds, maintaining a positive attitude and outlook, having a proper and balanced view of the world, maintaining a healthy lifestyle, having a sense of gratitude, having patience and perseverance, and living a life of moderation and avoiding extremes. These are all important components of achieving peace and contentment in life, and the Qur'an provides timeless guidance on how to achieve these goals.

27. Spiritual Growth: Awakening to the Qur'an's Wisdom

Spiritual growth is an important part of living according to the Qur'an in the modern times. This is because the Qur'an is a source of guidance and wisdom that can be used to help people grow spiritually.

The Qur'an is a reminder of Allah's guidance and mercy, and it is filled with deep spiritual truths that help us understand our place in the world and our relationship to Allah. The Qur'an is filled with reminders of the importance of faith, of being good to others, of seeking knowledge and understanding, of avoiding sin and striving for the highest ethical standards. It is a reminder of the importance of patience and perseverance, of understanding our own strengths and weaknesses and of striving to be the best we can be.

When we read the Qur'an, we can gain insight into our own spiritual path, and learn how to grow spiritually and reach our highest potential. The Qur'an helps us to develop a deeper understanding of our spiritual journey and the challenges we face along the way.

One of the most important aspects of spiritual growth is developing an understanding of the Qur'an and its teachings. We can do this by reading the Qur'an regularly, studying its meaning and reflecting on its teachings. This helps us to gain a better understanding of the spiritual truths contained in the Qur'an and how we can apply them to our lives.

The Qur'an also teaches us to remember Allah and to remain humble and thankful for all the blessings He has bestowed upon us. We should strive to be mindful of Allah throughout our lives and to always remember Him. The Qur'an encourages us to constantly strive to be better people and to live our lives in obedience to Allah's commands.

The Qur'an also teaches us the importance of prayer and supplication. Prayer is essential to our spiritual growth and development. Through prayer, we can seek Allah's guidance and mercy, ask for strength and guidance in our spiritual journey, and express our gratitude for all the blessings He has bestowed upon us.

The Qur'an also teaches us the importance of being good to others. We are reminded to be kind and compassionate to those around us, to be forgiving and merciful, and to always strive to do what is right. We should strive to be good examples to others, to help those in need and to make a positive contribution to society.

The Qur'an also encourages us to develop a sense of self-worth and to be proud of our faith and our identity as Muslims. We should strive to be proud of our Muslim heritage and to be proud of the values and beliefs that make us distinct from other religions and cultures.

The Qur'an also encourages us to strive for knowledge and to seek out wisdom and understanding. We should strive to learn more about our faith and to grow spiritually, to understand its teachings and to apply them to our lives.

How to Live by The Qur'an

Finally, the Qur'an encourages us to focus on the Hereafter and to be mindful of the consequences of our actions in this life. We should strive to be conscious of our actions and to ensure that they are in line with Allah's will.

By following the teachings of the Qur'an, we can grow spiritually and gain insight into the true nature of Allah and our purpose in life. The Qur'an is filled with reminders and spiritual truths that can help us to live our lives in accordance with Allah's will and to reach our highest potential as human beings. By embracing the spiritual truths contained in the Qur'an and applying them to our lives, we can gain a greater understanding of our spiritual journey and the challenges we face along the way.

28. The Importance of Charity in Building A Just And Fair Society

The Qur'an is clear that charity should be a part of our everyday lives and that it is essential to building a just and fair society. The Qur'an tells us that charity is a means of expressing our love for Allah and our commitment to Him. It is also a way of giving back to society and helping those in need.

The Qur'an states: *"And they give food, out of love for Him, to the needy, the orphan, and the captive, Saying: 'We feed you, for the sake of Allah, alone; we seek from you neither reward nor gratitude.'" (76:8-9).*

The Qur'an further explains the importance of charity by reminding us that we are all part of a greater community. It tells us that charity is not only for our own benefit, but for the benefit of all humanity. The Qur'an says: *"And those who spend their money in the cause of Allah, and do not follow up their gifts with reminders of their generosity or with injury, for them their reward is with their Lord; on them shall be no fear, nor shall they grieve." (2:262).*

This verse explains that when we give charity, we should do so without expecting anything in return. We should not be looking for recognition or to be praised for our good deeds, but instead we should be giving out of love and compassion for those in need.

The Qur'an also tells us that charity is an act of worship and that it is a source of spiritual growth. Part of the above quoted verse says : "Those who spend their wealth in the way of Allah, meaning that when we give charity, *we are doing an act of worship, and that it can help us to grow spiritually.* The act of giving charity is a way of showing our love and devotion to Allah, and of expressing our gratitude for His blessings.

The Qur'an also explains that charity should be given in a manner that is most beneficial to those in need. It tells us that charity should be given in a manner that is fair and just, and that it should not be given in a way that causes hardship or suffering to those in need. The Qur'an states: *"And those who give that which they give with their hearts full of fear, because they are sure to return to their Lord." (23:60).*

This verse explains that when we give charity, we should give it out of fear of Allah, and out of love for those in need. We should not give charity out of a desire for recognition or to be praised for our good deeds, but instead we should be giving out of a genuine concern for those in need.

Finally, the Qur'an reminds us that charity is essential in building a just and fair society. It tells us that charity should be given to those in need, regardless of their faith or background. The Qur'an states: *"O ye who believe! Spend of the good things which ye have earned, and of that which We have produced from the earth for you. And seek not the bad (with intent) to spend thereof (in charity) when ye would not take it for yourselves save with disdain; and know that Allah is Absolute, Owner of Praise." (2:267).*

This verse explains that charity should be given to those in need, regardless of their faith or background and we should be giving the best of the goods that we would like to enjoy ourselves and not the 'leftovers' which we will not like for ourselves. We should not be partial or discriminate when giving charity, but rather we should be giving it out of love and compassion for those in need.

In conclusion, charity is an integral part of our religious life and of building a just and fair society. The Qur'an tells us that we should not be looking for recognition or to be praised for our good deeds, but instead we should be giving out of love and a genuine concern for those in need. Charity is an act of worship, and it is essential in building a just and fair society. Turn yourself into a genuinely charitable person and see the magic. When you change, the society changes too.

29. The Qur'an and Science: Exploring the Wonders of the Universe

The Quran is a book of divine knowledge and guidance for mankind, and its teachings are timeless and universal. It is a book that encourages us to explore the wonders of the universe and to ponder over the grandeur of Allah's creation. The Quran also presents us with an opportunity to gain a deeper understanding of the relationship between our faith and the world around us. However, the Quran is, as it explains itself, a Book of Guidance' and not a book of science.

Nevertheless, it's a book of 'Signs' which fervently appeals our attentions to the surrounding natural phenomenon and many of its scientific facts baffled the scientists for ages. In this chapter, we will look at how the Quran and science intersect, and how the Quran can help us to explore the wonders of the universe. We will also examine how the Quran can provide us with an insight into the spiritual aspects of life and how to incorporate its teachings into our modern lives.

To begin with, let us consider the Quran's description of the universe. The Quran states that Allah created the universe in six 'days' and that He has perfect knowledge and control over all things. *And We did certainly create the heavens and earth and what is between them in six 'days', and there touched Us no weariness (Quran 50:38).* According to verse 70:3, one day in Quran is equal to 50,000 years of human counting on Earth. Therefore, Muslims interpret the description of a "six days" creation as seven distinct periods/ phases or eons. The Quran also states that He has placed stars and planets in the sky as signs for us to ponder over and to contemplate His power and greatness.

The Quran also mentions the importance of observation, discovery and exploration. It encourages us to observe the universe and to contemplate the wonders of Allah's creation. It also encourages us to explore the world around us and to gain knowledge from it. This is why the Quran encourages us to seek knowledge from the heavens and the earth.

However, the relationship between the Qur'an and science is a complex one, with many scholars offering various interpretations over the centuries. The Qur'an itself provides numerous invitations to explore the wonders of the universe and the scientific discoveries of our day often match with the descriptions given in the Qur'an. We may explore here some of the scientific aspects that are mentioned in the Qur'an and discuss how these discoveries can enrich our understanding of the Qur'an and its teachings.

As we said earlier, the Qur'an is not a book of science, but it contains many scientific facts and observations that were unknown or misunderstood at the time of its revelation. For example, the Qur'an mentions the spherical shape of the earth (Qur'an 79:30) and the fact that the sun and the moon both travel on their own orbits *(It is He Who created the night and the day, and the sun and the moon. Each of them is floating in its orbit. Qur'an 21:33)*. It also mentions the water cycle (*It is He who sends the winds as heralds of good news*

How to Live by The Qur'an

before His Mercy. We send down pure water from the sky, We certainly disperse it among them so they may be mindful, but most people persist in ungratefulness. (Qur'an 25:48-51) and the concept of continental drift. "And you see the mountains, thinking them rigid, while they will pass as the passing of clouds." (Surah An-Naml: 27:88)

If we focus on the verse, we can see that Allah says that our first thought would make us believe that mountains are fixed, and then we'll see that they are passing away as the passing of clouds. And it has been so exactly because only in the 19th century, we came to know that mountains could drift so could the continents. In another verse the Quran states *"As for the earth, We have stretched it out and placed on it firm mountains, and We have caused to grow in it everything well-balanced"* (Qur'an 15:19). All of these concepts were unknown when the Qur'an was revealed and thus can be seen as signs of its divine origin.

The Quran also speaks of the importance of scientific inquiry and encourages us to use our intellect and reason to gain knowledge. It states that the wise should strive to use their knowledge for the benefit of humanity and to create peace and harmony. This is why the Quran stresses the importance of science and scientific inquiry.

The Qur'an also describes the physical laws of nature in great detail. It mentions the concept of gravity (D*o you not see that Allah has subjected to you whatever is on the earth and the ships which run through the sea by His command? And <u>He restrains the sky from falling</u>*

Akhlaque Ahmed

upon the earth, unless by His permission. Indeed Allah, to the people, is Kind and Merciful. Qur'an 22:65). It also stresses the importance of the laws of nature, saying that everything in the universe is subject to these laws (Qur'an 11:7). *"and he (Allah) created everything, then ordained for it a measure. (Qur'an 25:2)"*. This is a piece of evidence that everything was created by Allah. Allah also said *"Everyone on it shall perish (or be destroyed) (Qur'an 55:26)*. This is a piece of evidence that everything shall be destroyed.

The Qur'an also describes the structure of the universe in great detail. It mentions the stars and planets, and their different orbits. There are two very important verses on the orbits of the Sun and Moon: *"(Allah is) the One Who created the night, the day, the sun and the moon. Each one is travelling in an orbit with its own motion." (Quran 21:33)* and in Surah Yasin: *"The sun must not catch up the moon, nor does the night outstrip the day. Each one is travelling in an orbit with its own motion." (Quran 36:40)*. Here an essential fact is clearly stated: the existence of the Sun's and Moon's orbits, plus a reference is made to the travelling of these bodies in space with their own motion.

The Qur'an also mentions the expanding nature of the universe (*The heaven, We have built it with power. Verily, We are expanding it."* Qur'an 51:47) and the fact that the universe is constantly changing and evolving. All of these concepts are now accepted by scientists and form the basis of modern cosmology.

The Qur'an also mentions the various stages of human development in great detail. It mentions the

How to Live by The Qur'an

creation of man from a single cell (Qur'an 23:12-14) and the stages of fetal development (Qur'an 22:5). It also mentions the development of the senses (Qur'an 17:36) and the importance of the human brain (Qur'an 41:53). All of these concepts are now accepted as fact by modern science.

In addition, the Qur'an also mentions the importance of observing and studying nature. It says that the study of nature is a way of understanding the divine will (Qur'an 3:190) and that the universe is filled with signs that point to the existence of Allah . *"n the heavens and the earth are proofs for the believers. And in your own creation, and in the creatures He scattered, are signs for people of firm faith. And in the alternation of night and day, and in the sustenance God sends down from the sky, with which He revives the earth after its death, and in the circulation of the winds, are marvels for people who reason."* (Qur'an 45:3-5). The Qur'an also encourages us to explore and discover the secrets of the universe. *Allah is the one who created seven heavens and from Earth like them (of the corresponding type); [Allah's] command descends among them (heavens and earth) so that you may know that Allah is capable of anything, and that Allah knows everything'.* (Quran 65:12). It makes us to think and ponder over universe beyond us.

The Qur'an also mentions the importance of maintaining balance and harmony in the universe. It says that Allah has created all things in pairs (*And from everything We have created pairs of twos, so that you may heed.* Qur'an 51:49) and that the universe is based on a system of balance. Everything we see around us, including our body, is created with very delicate balances. There is harmony in the heavens and on the earth and this harmony continued to exist without any disruption for millions of years. Allah makes all the systems of the universe function and grow in perfect harmony, even though, we are not aware of it. This concept of balance between physical forces is now a fundamental principle of modern science.

Finally, the Quran also speaks of the importance of understanding the spiritual aspects of life. It states that Allah has created the universe with a purpose, and that understanding this purpose is essential for our spiritual growth. This is why the Quran encourages us to use science to explore the spiritual aspects of life and to seek a deeper understanding of Allah's purpose. *No date-fruit comes out of its sheath, nor does a female conceive (within her womb) nor bring forth...' (Surat al Fussilat, 41:47).* As Allah states in this verse, He knows the every newborn human all around the World, He also knows all humans date of death in their destiny. Allah draws attention to this situation in the Quran: *'Nor does anyone know what it is that he will earn on tomorrow: Nor does anyone know in what land he is to die. Verily with Allah is full knowledge and He is acquainted (with all things).' (Surah al Luqman, 31:34).* This makes one to think deeply and invest in his spiritual self to find meaning and purpose in his life.

In conclusion, the Qur'an provides us with a unique insight into the physical laws of nature and the structure of the universe. It encourages us to observe and explore the wonders of the universe and to maintain balance and harmony in our lives. By studying the scientific aspects of the Qur'an, we can gain a deeper understanding of its teachings and how they can be applied in our modern world.

30. Serving Humanity: Working for Social Change

The Qur'an makes it clear that serving humanity is an integral part of living a life guided by Islamic principles. In fact, the Qur'an states that *"whoever works righteousness, whether male or female, while he (or she) is a true believer (of Islamic faith), verily, to him We will give a good life (in this world with respect, contentment, and lawful provision) and We shall pay them certainly a reward in proportion to the best of what they used to do (i.e. Paradise in the Hereafter)" (Qur'an 16:97)*.

This verse highlights the importance of serving humanity in Islam. The Qur'an emphasizes that service to humanity is not only a spiritual obligation, but also a way to obtain material blessings and rewards in this world and the hereafter. This means that those who work for the benefit of humanity will receive their due reward in this life and the next.

This chapter will discuss the importance of serving humanity, as well as practical ways to do so in the modern times. It will also discuss how Islamic principles can be applied to work for social change.

I. The Qur'an on Serving Humanity

The Qur'an emphasizes the importance of serving humanity in various ways. *Serve Allah and ascribe no partner to Him. Do good to your parents, to near of kin, to orphans, and to the needy, and to the neighbour who is of kin and to the neighbour who is a stranger, and to the companion by your side, and to the wayfarer, and to those whom your right hands possess. (Qur'an 4:36)*.

How to Live by The Qur'an

Here Allah first says to worship Him alone, and then to serve a long list of people. This is showing that to serve being kind is an act of worship. The first groups on this list are parents and relatives It mentions that those who are kind and compassionate to their fellow humans will enter Paradise (Qur'an 4:36). The Qur'an also mentions that those who help the needy, orphans, and the poor will receive reward from Allah (Qur'an 2:177). The Qur'an also states that those who give financially to the poor are "like a grain of corn that grows seven ears, in every ear a hundred grains" (Qur'an 2:261).

Not only does the Qur'an emphasize the importance of giving charity but also of helping those in need in many other ways. The Qur'an states that those who "invite to the way of your Lord (i.e. Islam) with wisdom and fair preaching, and argue with them in a way that is better" (Qur'an 16:125) are among the righteous. The Qur'an also mentions those who strive to bring about justice and peace in society, stating "those who strive hard for Us (Our Cause), We will surely guide them to Our Paths (i.e. Allah's Religion - Islamic Monotheism)" (Qur'an 29:69).

The Qur'an also encourages believers to help their neighbors, stating "and worship Allah and associate none with Him (in worship); and do good to parents, kinsfolk, orphans, Al-Masaakeen (the poor), the neighbour who is near of kin, the neighbour who is a stranger, the companion by your side, the wayfarer (you meet), and those (slaves) whom your right hands possess" (Qur'an 4:36).

The Qur'an also encourages believers to be patient and perseverant in serving humanity, stating "verily, Allah is with those who are As-Saabiroon (the patient)" (Qur'an 2:153). This is an important reminder that serving humanity is not an easy task and requires patience and perseverance.

II. Practical Ways to Serve Humanity

There are many practical ways to serve humanity in the modern times. One of the most important ways is to help those in need. This includes providing financial help, food, clothing, and other necessities to those who are less fortunate. This can be done through charitable organizations or by directly providing assistance to those in need.

Another way to serve humanity is to volunteer in various social service initiatives. This can include volunteering in homeless shelters, soup kitchens, or any other service organization that provides aid to those in need.

Educating others about social issues and helping to spread awareness is also an important way to serve humanity. This can be done by engaging in conversations about social issues, writing articles or blog posts about them, or by organizing events that raise awareness about social problems.

Another way to serve humanity is to take part in social movements and campaigns. This can include joining protests against injustice, participating in letter writing campaigns, or engaging in other forms of advocacy work.

Finally, one of the most important ways to serve humanity is to be kind and compassionate to others. This includes treating others with respect, being open to listening to the perspectives of those who are different from us, and engaging in acts of kindness and generosity.

III. Working for Social Change

Working for social change is an important way to serve humanity in the modern times. It is important to remember that social change is a slow process and requires dedication and perseverance.

One of the most important principles of social change is to work for justice and peace. This means standing up for those who are disadvantaged or oppressed, advocating for laws that protect the rights of all people, and standing against any injustice.

It is also important to be aware of the root causes of social problems. This includes understanding the history, culture, and socio-economic conditions that lead to particular issues. This knowledge can be used to create effective strategies to work for social change.

It is also important to be creative in working for social change. This can involve thinking outside the box and coming up with innovative ideas to address social problems.

Finally, it is important to remember that working for social change is not a one-person effort. It is important to build strong coalitions with others who are working for the same cause. Working together and pooling resources can be an effective way to create lasting social change.

Akhlaque Ahmed

Serving humanity is an important part of living a life guided by Islamic principles. The Qur'an emphasizes the importance of helping those in need, engaging in acts of kindness and compassion, and working for justice and peace. These principles can be applied in practical ways to serve humanity in the modern times. This includes providing assistance to those in need, educating others about social issues, and working for social change. By taking part in these activities, one can help make a difference in the world and obtain rewards both in this life and the hereafter.

31. Forgiveness and Mercy: Embracing the Qur'an's Message

One of the primary messages of the Qur'an is that of mercy and forgiveness. This message is emphasized throughout the Qur'an and is essential to living by its teachings in modern times. The mercy and forgiveness that Allah offers through the Qur'an is an integral part of Islamic beliefs and practices and can be seen in how Muslims strive to live their lives.

The Qur'an emphasizes the importance of forgiveness and mercy in multiple verses. In Surah Al-Ma'idah, verse 8, it is stated, *"O you who have believed, be persistently standing firm in justice, witnesses for Allah, even if it be against yourselves or parents and relatives. Whether one is rich or poor, Allah is more worthy of both. So follow not [personal] inclination, lest you not be just. And if you distort [your testimony] or refuse [to give it], then indeed Allah is ever, with what you do, Acquainted."* This verse emphasizes that justice must be practiced in any situation and that personal desires should be set aside for the greater good. This includes being forgiving and merciful to others, regardless of who they are.

In other verses, Allah speaks of His mercy and forgiveness. In Surah Al-Shurah, verse 37, Allah states, *"And those who avoid the major sins and immoralities, and when they are angry, they forgive."* This verse emphasizes the importance of controlling anger and being forgiving even when one is angry. In Surah Al-Nisa, verse 110, Allah speaks of His own mercy and forgiveness, stating, *"And whoever does a wrong or wrongs himself but then seeks forgiveness of Allāh will find Allāh Forgiving and Merciful."* In another verse Allah says *And ask forgiveness of your Lord and then repent to Him. Indeed, my Lord is Merciful and Affectionate." (Quran 11:90)* These two verses emphasizes the importance of Allah's forgiveness and mercy towards His creations.

The importance of mercy and forgiveness is also seen in the Islamic concept of *Taqwa,* or Allah-consciousness. Taqwa is a state of mind in which one is constantly aware of Allah and His presence. In this state of mind, one is more likely to live in a way that pleases Allah, which includes being forgiving and merciful. In Surah Al-Hujurat, verse 13, Allah states, *"O humankind, We have created you from a male and a female, and made you into nations and tribes, that you may know one another. Indeed, the most noble of you in the sight of Allah is the most Allah-conscious of you." (Quran 49:13).* This verse emphasizes the importance of being conscious of Allah and living in a way that pleases Him so that we can deserve His mercy.

The concept of forgiveness and mercy is also seen in the Islamic practice of fasting during the month of Ramadan. During this month, Muslims fast as a way of showing their devotion to Allah and seeking His forgiveness and mercy. In Surah Al-Baqarah, verse 183, Allah states, *"O you who have believed, decreed upon you is fasting as it was decreed upon those before you that you may become Allah-conscious."* This verse emphasizes the importance of fasting in order to become

How to Live by The Qur'an

more conscious of Allah and seek His mercy and forgiveness.

The importance of mercy and forgiveness is also seen in the Islamic concept of zakat, or charity. Zakat is one of the five pillars of Islam and is a way for Muslims to give back to their communities and to demonstrate their faith in Allah. In Surah At-Tawbah, verse 60, Allah states, *"Take from their wealth a charity by which you purify them and cause them increase, and invoke Allah's blessings upon them. Indeed, your invocations are reassurance for them."* This verse emphasizes the importance of giving charity in order to purify oneself and seek Allah's mercy and blessings.

The concept of mercy and forgiveness is also seen in the Islamic practice of salat, or prayer. Salat is one of the five pillars of Islam and is a way for Muslims to demonstrate their faith in Allah and seek His mercy and forgiveness. In Surah Al-Baqarah, verse 186, Allah states, "And when My servants ask you concerning Me, then surely, I am near. I answer the prayer of the supplicant when he calls on Me. So let them obey Me and believe in Me, that they may be led aright." This verse emphasizes the importance of prayer in seeking Allah's mercy and forgiveness.

Finally, the concept of mercy and forgiveness is also seen in the Islamic practice of hajj, or pilgrimage. Hajj is one of the five pillars of Islam and is a way for Muslims to demonstrate their faith in Allah and seek His mercy and forgiveness. In Surah Al-Hajj, verse 27, Allah states, "And proclaim to the people the Hajj [pilgrimage]; they will come to you on foot and on every lean camel, they will come from every deep and distant [wide] mountain highway." This verse emphasizes the importance of the Hajj as a way to seek Allah's mercy and forgiveness.

In conclusion, mercy and forgiveness are essential aspects of living by the Qur'an in modern times. These concepts are emphasized throughout the Qur'an and are seen in various Islamic beliefs and practices. By living according to these principles, Muslims can demonstrate their faith in Allah and seek His mercy and forgiveness. Ultimately, mercy and forgiveness are essential aspects of living a life in accordance with the teachings of the Qur'an.

32. The Power of Prayer: Connecting with the Divine

The power of prayer can never be underestimated in one's life. Prayer is an essential part of the Muslim faith, and it is an essential part of life for all believers. Prayer is a form of communication between a person and Allah, and it is a way to connect with the divine. In the Qur'an, Allah states: "And your Lord says: "Call on Me; I will answer your prayer" (Qur'an 40:60). This verse is a reminder to all believers that Allah hears our prayers and answers them.

In the modern times, many people have forgotten the power of prayer and how to use it to connect with the divine. In this chapter, we will discuss the power of prayer and how to use it to connect with the divine. We will also discuss the importance of prayer and how it can help us in our daily lives.

The power of prayer is derived from its simplicity and the fact that it requires nothing but faith and sincerity. Prayer is an act of worship and it is a way to express our love and gratitude to the Creator. Prayer is not only a way to ask for something, but it is also a way to thank Allah for all of the blessings He has bestowed upon us.

When we pray, we should be mindful of the words we are saying and the intention behind our words. Prayer should be done with humility and sincerity, and we should be mindful of the words that we are using. We should also be mindful of the timing and place of our prayer. Praying at the appropriate time and place will increase the chances of our prayer being answered.

Prayer can be used to ask Allah for guidance, protection, and help in our day-to-day lives. Through prayer, we can ask Allah to guide us in our decision-making and help us to stay on the right path. We can also ask Allah for protection against any harm or danger that may come our way.

Prayer can also be used to ask Allah for forgiveness and to repent for our sins. We can use prayer to ask Allah for His mercy and forgiveness, and to guide us to the right path. We can also use prayer to ask Allah to grant us inner peace and contentment.

Prayer can also be used to ask Allah for strength and courage when we are facing difficult times. We can use prayer to ask Allah for the strength and courage to face our fears and to remain firm in our faith. We can also use prayer to ask Allah for wisdom and to help us understand the truth.

The power of prayer can also be used to ask Allah for health and healing. We can use prayer to ask Allah to grant us physical and mental health. We can also use prayer to ask Allah to help us in our struggle against any illness or disease.

Finally, the power of prayer can be used to ask Allah for wealth and prosperity. We can use prayer to ask Allah to grant us financial stability and to provide us with the means to live a comfortable life. We can also use prayer to ask Allah for blessings in our lives and for success in all of our endeavors.

How to Live by The Qur'an

In conclusion, prayer is an essential part of the Muslim faith and it is a powerful tool to connect with the divine. Prayer can be used to ask Allah for guidance, protection, strength, and healing. We should always be mindful of the words we are using and the intention behind them. When we pray with sincerity and humility, Allah will surely answer our prayers.

33: Making the Most of Faith In The Modern World

The world today is changing, and with it, the challenges faced by those of us who wish to live by the teachings of the Quran and Sunnah. The question of how to make the most of our faith in the modern world is an increasingly relevant one. The Quran and Sunnah provide us with an invaluable source of guidance on how to live according to the will of Allah, and this guidance can be applied to our everyday lives in order to make the most of our faith in the modern world.

In this chapter, we will focus on five key areas of action that can help us make the most of our faith in the modern world: living a life of gratitude and remembrance of Allah, learning to be content, striving for knowledge, developing a sense of community, and supporting social justice.

Living a life of gratitude and remembrance of Allah

Living a life of gratitude and remembrance of Allah is one of the most important aspects of living according to the teachings of the Quran and Sunnah. This entails constantly making an effort to be mindful of Allah and to express gratitude for His blessings. As Allah says in the Quran:

"So remember Me and I shall remember you; give thanks to Me and do not be ungrateful to Me for My favours." (Quran 2:152).

This verse emphasizes the importance of remembering Allah and expressing gratitude for His blessings. We can do this by regularly reciting the Quran, making du'a (supplications), and thanking Allah for all the blessings He has bestowed upon us. Doing this on a regular basis will help us to stay connected to Allah and to remain mindful of His presence in our lives.

Learning to be content

Another key aspect of making the most of our faith in the modern world is learning to be content. The world today is full of distractions that can easily lead us astray if we are not careful. This is why it is important to learn to be content with what Allah has given us, and to be grateful for the blessings He has bestowed upon us. In the Quran, Allah says:

"And give the relative his due, and [also] the poor and the traveler, and do not spend wastefully. Indeed, the wasteful are brothers of the devils, and ever has Satan been to his Lord ungrateful" (Quran 17:26-27).

This verse emphasizes the importance of being content with what Allah has given us and not wasting our time and resources on things that are not beneficial. By learning to be content and being grateful for the blessings we have been given, we can make the most of our faith in the modern world.

Striving for knowledge

In the modern world, knowledge is increasingly important. Being knowledgeable about the teachings of the Quran and Sunnah is essential for those of us who wish to make the most of our faith. The Prophet Muhammad (PBUH) said: *"Seeking knowledge is an obligation upon every Muslim" (Tirmidhi).*

This hadith emphasizes the importance of striving for knowledge in order to make the most of our faith in the modern world. We can do this by regularly reading the Quran and Sunnah, attending Islamic classes and conferences, and engaging in meaningful discussions about Islamic topics with like-minded people.

Developing a sense of community

Living in the modern world can be isolating and it can be easy to become disconnected from our faith if we are not careful. This is why it is important to develop a sense of community and to connect with other Muslims. The Prophet Muhammad (PBUH) said: *"The believers are like one body; when one limb complains, the rest of the body responds with wakefulness and fever" (Muslim).*

This hadith emphasizes the importance of developing a sense of community and of looking out for one another. We can do this by attending Islamic events and gatherings, joining Islamic organizations, and getting involved in local community initiatives.

Supporting social justice

Finally, we must strive to support social justice in the modern world. Social justice is an important part of living according to the teachings of the Quran and Sunnah. Allah says in the Quran:

"O you who have believed, be persistently standing firm in justice, witnesses for Allah, even if it be against yourselves or parents and relatives. Whether one is rich or poor, Allah is more worthy of both. So follow not [personal] inclination, lest you not be just. And if you distort [your testimony] or refuse [to give it], then indeed Allah is ever, with what you do, Acquainted" (Quran 4:135).

This verse emphasizes the importance of standing up for justice even if it goes against our own interests. We can do this by speaking out against injustice, supporting those who are oppressed, and taking action to address social issues.

In conclusion, living by the teachings of the Quran and Sunnah in the modern world is not always easy. There are many challenges that we must face and many obstacles that we must overcome. However, by following the five key areas of action outlined in this chapter, we can make the most of our faith in the modern world. By living a life of gratitude and remembrance of Allah, learning to be content, striving for knowledge, developing a sense of community, and supporting social justice, we can make the most of our faith in the modern world and strive to live according to the will of Allah.

34: Useful tips and concluding remarks

The teachings of Quran provide us with a comprehensive guide to help us lead a purposeful and meaningful life. All of us have a different life journey and we have to use the teachings of Quran to take the right decisions and make the right choices. This chapter will provide some useful tips and concluding remarks to help us live a life by following the teachings of the Quran.

Tips to Live a Life by the Teachings of Quran

1. Read the Quran Regularly:

It is important to read the Quran regularly and in a consistent manner. We should aim to read the Quran at least once a day, or even twice a day if possible. This helps us to keep track of our progress and ensure that we are following the teachings of the Quran. We should also take time to reflect on the verses of the Quran, and ponder over the meanings and explanations of the verses.

2. Practise What You Preach:

It is important to practise what you preach and follow the teachings of the Quran in your everyday lives. We should not just read the Quran, but also strive to put the teachings into practice. We should strive to be kind and compassionate, honest and truthful, and always aim to do good deeds and help others.

3. Make Dua:

We should make Dua to Allah regularly and sincerely. Dua is an important aspect of our faith, and it is through Dua that we can communicate our thoughts

How to Live by The Qur'an

and feelings to Allah. We should seek guidance, ask for help and forgiveness, and express our gratitude to Allah.

4. Seek Knowledge:

We should strive to seek knowledge and increase our understanding of the Quran. We should attend religious classes, listen to lectures, and read books on the Quran to increase our knowledge. We should also learn the proper recitation of the Quran, and strive to understand the meanings of the verses.

5. Be Patient and Perseverant:

We should strive to be patient and perseverant in our journey of following the teachings of the Quran. We should not expect immediate results, but rather strive to continue on our path and trust in the will of Allah. We should also remember that patience and perseverance are essential in order to achieve any goal.

6. Have Faith and Believe in Allah:

We should strive to have faith and believe in Allah. We should trust that Allah knows what is best for us and that He will always provide us with the best outcomes. We should also remember that Allah is always with us and that He will never leave us alone.

7. Surround Yourself with Positive People and Environments:

We should strive to surround ourselves with positive people and environments. This will help us to stay on the right path and ensure that we are following the teachings of the Quran. We should also avoid negative influences and strive to be positive in our thoughts and actions.

8. Seek Help from Others:

We should not be afraid to seek help from others if we are struggling to follow the teachings of the Quran. We should not be ashamed to ask for help and advice and should strive to seek guidance from knowledgeable people. We should also remember that Allah is always with us, and that He will always provide us with the strength and courage to continue on our journey.

Following the teachings of the Quran can be difficult, especially in today's modern world. However, with patience, perseverance and faith, we can overcome any obstacle and strive to live a life by the teachings of the Quran. We should also remember that we are not alone in our journey and that Allah is always with us, guiding us and providing us with the strength and courage to continue.

We can also take inspiration from the life of famous celebrities who have found peace in Islam, such as Muhammad Ali and Yusuf Islam. These celebrities have shown us that it is possible to live a life following the teachings of the Quran, even in a modern world.

In conclusion, it is important to remember that the teachings of the Quran provide us with a comprehensive guide to help us lead a purposeful and meaningful life. We should strive to read the Quran regularly, practise what we preach, make Dua, and seek knowledge. We should also be patient and perseverant, have faith and believe in Allah, surround ourselves with positive people and environments, and seek help from others. May Allah make your journey easy and fulfilling.

References

Nasr, Seyyed Hossein (2015) *The Study Quran: A New Translation and Commentary*- HarperOne.

Wills, Garry (2017) *What the Qur'an Meant And Why It Matters*: Penguin Publishing Group

Cook, Michael, *The Koran: a very short introduction*, Oxford: Oxford University Press, 2000.

Mattson, Ingrid, *The Story of the Qur'an: Its History and Place in Muslim Life*, Malden: Blackwell, 2008.

M. A. S. Abdel Haleem, *The Qur'an: An English Translation with Parallel Arabic Text*, Oxford: Oxford University Press, 2004.

Al-Munajjid, S. (2003). *Understanding Islam: A Guide for New Muslims*. Riyadh, Saudi Arabia: Darussalam Publications.

An-Nawawi, M. (2001). *Forty Hadiths*. Beirut, Lebanon: Dar Al-Fikr.

Asad, M. (2003). *The Message of The Qur'an*. Gibraltar: Dar al-Andalus.

Esposito, J. L. (2002). *What Everyone Needs to Know About Islam*. Oxford, UK: Oxford University Press.

Saeed, A. (2006). *The Qur'an: An Introduction*. London, UK: Routledge.

Glossary

A glossary of Islamic Terms

'Adl: Justice; fairness and equity.

'Aql: Reason; the ability to think and make sound judgments.

'Ibadah: Worship; the act of serving Allah.

Aayat: A verse in the Quran.

Adab: Respect and courtesy; proper behavior towards others.

Ahl al-Kitab: People of the Book, referring to followers of other Abrahamic religions.

Akhirah: The Day of Judgment, when all souls will be judged by Allah.

Akhlaq: Morality; good character and behavior.

Al-Aqeedah: Islamic beliefs; the fundamental articles of faith in Islam. Beliefs and doctrines of Islam.

Al-Aqsa Mosque: The third holiest site in Islam, located in Jerusalem.

Al-Hadeeth: The sayings and actions of Prophet Muhammad (peace be upon him).

Allah: The one and only Allah.

Al-Quran: The holy book of Islam, the actual words of Allah as revealed to Prophet Muhammad (peace be upon him).

Amal: Action; deeds done by a person.

Amanah: Trustworthiness and responsibility.

Amr bil Ma'ruf: Commanding good; the obligation to enjoin what is right and forbid what is wrong.

Ashab al-Yahud: People of the Jewish faith.

Asma al-Husna: The 99 beautiful names of Allah.

Athaab: Punishment from Allah.

Athar: A saying of a Companion of the Prophet Muhammad (peace be upon him).

Awrah: Areas of the body which must be covered, particularly in the presence of non-mahrams.

Ayah: A verse in the Quran.

Bara'ah: Disassociation; the act of publicly disavowing a person or group.

Barakah: Blessing, which can be obtained through obedience to Allah.

Barzakh: The intermediate realm between this world and the Hereafter.

Bidah: An innovation in religious practice not sanctioned by the Quran or Sunnah.

Bismillah: The opening phrase of the Quran, meaning "In the name of Allah".

Da'wah: Inviting people to the truth of Islam.

Dar al-Harb: The House of War, referring to non-Muslim countries.

Dar al-Islam: The House of Islam, referring to Muslim countries.

Dar al-Sulh: Dar Al Sulh, or Domain of Conciliation, is a territory where an agreement between Muslims and non-Muslims has been made and provides freedom of religion, autonomy, and protection. Lit. meaning 'abode of the Truce

Dawah: Inviting people to follow the teachings of Islam.

Dhabh: Animal sacrifice.

Dharurah: Necessity; something so important that it overrides all other considerations.

Dhikr: Remembrance of Allah; the act of mentioning or thinking of Allah, by repeating phrases such as Allahu Akbar (Allah is Great).

Du'a: A prayer to Allah, asking for His help and guidance.

Fard: Obligation; an act that is obligatory in Islamic law.

Fiqh al-Akbar: The most important Islamic jurisprudence.

Fiqh: Islamic jurisprudence, i.e. the science of interpreting Islamic law.

Fitrah: The natural state of a human being, created by Allah.

Ghaflah: Negligence in worship.

Hadith Qudsi: A saying of Allah, revealed to the Prophet Muhammad, but not incorporated in the Qur'an.

Hadith: A report of the sayings and actions of the Prophet Muhammad (peace be upon him).

Hajj: The Islamic pilgrimage to Mecca.

Hajjah: Reason; a valid cause for a legal ruling.

Halal: Permissible; something allowed in Islam.

Haram: Forbidden; something not allowed in Islam.

Haya: Modesty and shyness, which is highly praised in Islam.

How to Live by The Qur'an

Hijab: A veil or head covering worn by Muslim women.

Hisab: Reckoning; being held accountable for one's deeds.

Hudud: The punishments prescribed by Islamic law, such as stoning for adultery.

Husn al-Khulq: Good manners; proper behaviour towards others.

Ibadah: Worship of Allah.

Ihsan: Excellence; Doing righteous deeds to the best of one's ability.

Ihtiyat: Precaution; taking extra care to ensure that something is done correctly.

Ijma al-Ummah: Consensus of the ummah; the agreement of the majority of the Muslim community on a point of law.

Ijma: Consensus of Islamic scholars on a certain point of law.

Ijma': Consensus; the agreement of a group of scholars on a point of law.

Ijtihad: The process of using independent reasoning to reach a conclusion on a point of Islamic law.

Ilm: Knowledge, which is a key part of worship.

Imam: A spiritual leader in the Islamic faith.

Iman: Belief; faith in the unseen.

Injil: The Gospel, revealed to Jesus.

Insha'Allah: "Allah willing", often used to express the hope that something will happen.

Iqama: The call to prayer.

Istighfar: Seeking forgiveness from Allah.

Istihsab: Presumption; the inference of something from circumstantial evidence.

Istihsan: Preference; the use of discretion in determining a legal ruling.

Istishhad: Martyrdom, or sacrificing one's life in the way of Allah.

Istislah: Public interest; the collective benefit of the Muslim community. The process of deducing Islamic law based on public interest.

Ittiba: Following the example of the Prophet Muhammad.

Jahannam: Hell; the abode of the wicked in the Hereafter.

Jama'ah: A community of believers.

Jannah: Heaven, a reward for those who obey Allah. Paradise; the abode of the righteous in the Hereafter.

Jihad al-Nafs: Striving against one's own desires and temptations.

Jihad: A struggle in the path of Allah; the term can refer to both inner and outer struggles.

Ka'aba: The cube-shaped building at the centre of the Masjid al-Haram in Mecca.

Kaffarah: A form of expiation, such as fasting, for certain sins.

Karamah: Miracle; a supernatural act attributed to Allah or one of His prophets.

Khayr: Good; something of benefit.

Khilafah: Leadership; the right to rule. A Muslim state, ruled by an Islamic leader. Also, Succession; the right to rule after the death of a ruler.

Kufr: Disbelief in Allah and His teachings.

Lailat al-Qadr: The Night of Power, when the Quran was first revealed.

Ma'a: Social justice and fairness.

Ma'ruf: Righteous and good deeds.

Mahabbah: Love; a feeling of intense affection.

Mahr: A mandatory payment given by a groom to his bride upon marriage.

Mahram: A family member with whom marriage is forbidden.

Mahzab: School of thought; a particular interpretation of Islamic law.

Marifah: Knowing Allah.

Masjid: A mosque, where Muslims can gather to perform prayer and worship.

Maslahah: Common good; the collective benefit of the Muslim community.

Mu'min: A believer in Allah.

Mubah: Neutral; something that is neither halal nor haram.

Mubahala: A form of prayer and supplication to Allah, involving a group of people.

Mufti: An Islamic legal scholar, who provides rulings on matters of Islamic law.

Muharram: The first month of the Islamic calendar.

Mujtahid: A scholar who is qualified to exercise ijtihad.

Munafiq: A hypocrite, who claims to be a believer but does not act according to the teachings of Islam.

Munafiq: Hypocrite; a person who outwardly professes to be a believer but inwardly has another agenda.

Munafiqun: Hypocrites, who claim to be believers but do not act according to the teachings of Islam.

Murabahah: A form of financing in which a buyer agrees to purchase a commodity at a price higher than the cost of the item.

Mustahab: An act that is recommended by Islamic scholars, but not obligatory.

Nabi: A prophet.

Nafs: The human soul.

Nahy 'anil Munkar: Prohibiting evil; the obligation to stand against what is wrong and corrupt.

Naskh: The process of abrogating an earlier ruling with a later one.

Ni'mah: Blessing; something of benefit given by Allah.

Qiblah: The direction of prayer, which is towards the Ka'aba in Mecca.

Qira'at: The various ways of reading the Quran.

Qiyamah: The Day of Judgment; the day when all will be judged by Allah for their deeds.

Qiyas: Analogy; drawing a legal ruling from an existing precedent.

Qur'an: The holy book of Islam, revealed to the Prophet Muhammad.

Quranic Arabic: The language of the Quran, which is a distinct form of Arabic.

Rasul: A messenger; a prophet with a revealed scripture.

Riba: Usury or interest, which is forbidden in Islam.

Rida: Contentment; acceptance of the decrees and decisions of Allah.

Risalah: A letter or message sent by the Prophet Muhammad.

Risalah: Message; a communication from Allah to humans.

Sabr: Patience and perseverance in the face of adversity.

Sadaqah: Voluntary charity, given without any expectation of reward.

Salat: Islamic prayer; a ritual prayer performed five times a day.

Sawm: Islamic fasting; abstaining from food, drink and sexual relations during the daylight hours of Ramadan.

Sha'riah: Islamic law derived from the Quran and Sunnah.

Shaf'a: Intercession on behalf of another person on the Day of Judgment.

Shafa'ah: Intercession; the act of asking Allah to forgive sins and grant mercy.

Shari'ah Court: A court of Islamic law, where disputes are settled according to the Quran and Sunnah.

Shari'ah: Islamic law, based on the Quran and Sunnah.

Shirk: Associating partners with Allah; the worst sin.

Shuf'ah: Sincerity; the act of making sincere efforts to do something.

Shukr: Gratitude to Allah for His blessings.

Sifah: Characteristics; the attributes of Allah.

Sujud: Prostration, which is an important part of prayer.

Sulh: Reconciliation; making peace.

Sunnah: Custom; The teachings and practices of the Prophet Muhammad (peace be upon him).

Surah: A chapter of the Quran.

Ta'zir: A punishment which is not prescribed in Islamic law, but is imposed by a judge in a court of law.

Tahara: Purity of body and soul, which is necessary for worship.

Tahir: Clean, which is necessary for prayer and other acts of worship.

Taqiyyah: Dissimulation; concealing one's true beliefs in order to preserve life or property.

Taqwa: Fear of Allah and being conscious of His presence.

Taubah: Repentance.

Tawakkul: Reliance; the act of trusting in Allah and relying on Him.

Tawassul: Seeking the intercession of the Prophet Muhammad (peace be upon him).

Tawbah: Repentance; turning to Allah in sincere regret and resolve to change.

Thawab: Spiritual reward for righteous deeds.

How to Live by The Qur'an

Ulema: A scholar of Islamic studies.

Ummah: The global Muslim community. The Muslim community worldwide.

Ummahat al-Mu'mineen: The Mothers of the Believers, referring to the wives of the Prophet Muhammad.

Wajib: Necessity; an act that is necessary for the performance of an obligation.

Wala': Loyalty; a feeling of closeness and attachment to one's family and community.

Waqf: An endowment or trust, which is used to support a charitable cause.

Wasiyyah: A will, which can be made to distribute one's wealth after death.

Wazifah: A special form of remembrance of Allah, involving the recitation of certain phrases.

Wudhu: Ablution performed before prayer.

Yawm al-Qiyamah: The Day of Resurrection, when all souls will be judged.

Zabihah: Slaughtering an animal for the purpose of food, in accordance with Islamic law.

Zakat: Islamic charity; an obligatory charity payable by those who have the means.

Zina: Adultery or fornication, which is forbidden in Islam.

Akhlaque Ahmed

Notes

How to Live by The Qur'an

Notes

Printed in Great Britain
by Amazon